What People Are Saying

"I have known Peter Biadasz in a variety of capacities for many years. From networking guru to reliable sounding board, Peter's knowledge and skill never ceases to amaze me. Efficient and effective from the board room to the golf course. Very few professionals rival Peter's mastery of life."

Melissa Randolph
Director of Sales and Marketing
Cypress Golf Solutions

"Matt Eidson has always been a man of style and substance. Matt's original approach to sales (and golf) makes the ordinary extraordinary. Matt is delightfully entertaining."

Melissa Randolph
Director of Sales and Marketing
Cypress Golf Solutions

"There are great networkers and there are great salespeople ... all too often in today's business environment they are mutually exclusive. Peter is one of those people who has effectively integrated both sides of the success coin and uses it flawlessly in his talks, in his writings and his dealings with people. If you are struggling in your own business, I strongly suggest listening closely to this man ... I do."

Adam J. Kovitz, The National Networker

"Golf and life are much alike: you get out of each one what you are willing to put into both. If you work smart, not hard, you will receive great benefits."

Edd Dennis, Territory Mgr for Tour Edge Golf and former club/teaching pro.

(See inside back cover for more endorsements)

Increase Your Sales
And
Lower Your Golf Score

**Library Commons
Georgian College
One Georgian Drive
Barrie, ON
L4M 3X9**

HF5438.4 .B53 2007
0134110521769
Biadasz, Peter.

Increase your sales and
 lower your golf score :
    c2007.

2008 01 30

Increase Your Sales And Lower Your Golf Score

Everything you need to know about sales you can learn by playing golf

Peter Biadasz and Matt Eidson

iUniverse, Inc.
New York Lincoln Shanghai

Increase Your Sales And Lower Your Golf Score
Everything you need to know about sales you can learn by playing golf

Copyright © 2007 by Peter Biadasz and Matt Eidson

All rights reserved. No part of this book may be used or reproduced by any means, graphic, electronic, or mechanical, including photocopying, recording, taping or by any information storage retrieval system without the written permission of the publisher except in the case of brief quotations embodied in critical articles and reviews.

iUniverse books may be ordered through booksellers or by contacting:

iUniverse
2021 Pine Lake Road, Suite 100
Lincoln, NE 68512
www.iuniverse.com
1-800-Authors (1-800-288-4677)

The views expressed in this work are solely those of the author and do not necessarily reflect the views of the publisher, and the publisher hereby disclaims any responsibility for them.

ISBN: 978-0-595-43783-2 (pbk)
ISBN: 978-0-595-88113-0 (ebk)

Printed in the United States of America

This book is dedicated to the many people that have believed in me through the years. Thank you!!! It is because of you that many others are being affected in a positive way.

—Peter Biadasz

I would like to dedicate this book to my children. They inspire me to improve myself every single day. I would also like to thank my co-author Peter Biadasz for encouraging me to pursue this project and being patient while I completed it.

—Matt Eidson

Contents

Why Read This book? xxi

Acknowledgements xxiii

Foreword xxv

Introduction xxvii
- You Need This Book If xxvii
- How This Book is Organized xxvii
- How To Use This Book xxix

Chapter 1
The Salesperson and the Golfer—Our Story Begins 1

Chapter 2
Preparation—The Making of a Professional 3
A. Determine Your Level of Dedication 4
    Sales 4
    1. Life Goals 4
    2. Income 5
    Golf 6
    1. What Is Your Level Of Dedication? 6
    2. Be The Best You Can Be 6

B. Effective Use Of Practice Time/Become A Student Of The Game 7
    Sales 7
    1. Lack of Knowledge Will Cost You $$$$$ 7
    2. Practice Every Part of the Sales Cycle 7
    Golf 8
    1. Make Sure You Practice the Right Things 8
    2. Be Dedicated to Improvement 8

C. Etiquette 9
    Sales 9
    1. How You Treat Yourself 9
    2. How You Treat Others 9
    Golf 9
    1. Keep Up a Good Pace of Play 10
    2. Proper Manners on the Tee Box, In the Fairway, On the Green, and In the Clubhouse 10

D. Equipment 12
    Sales 12
    1. Your Brain (Attitude—Your Most Important Asset) 12
    2. Your Education 14
    3. Your Appearance 14
    4. Your "Sales Ball" 14
    5. The Inner Game Of Sales 15
        a. Self Motivation 15
        b. Independence 15
        c. Professionalism 16

  Golf..16
   1. Custom Fitting...16
   2. Choosing the Right Woods, Irons, Wedges, Putter, Golf Ball and Tee...17
   3. Care and Maintenance...20
   4. Different Equipment for Different Courses or Conditions 20
 E. Knowledge of the Course..21
  Sales..21
   1. Your Product/Service/Company 21
   2. Your Industry 21
   3. Your Target Market/Prospects 22
   4. Your Competition 22
  Golf..23
   1. Course Rating and Slope Rating...23
   2. Architectural Tendencies..23
   3. Geography, Climate and Grass Type..24
   4. Local Knowledge...25
 F. Warm Up Routine..25
  Sales..26
   1. Effectively Starting Your Sales Day...26
   2. Goals..26
   3. Sleep..26
  Golf..27
   1. Range...27
   2. Chipping Green and Practice Bunker..27
   3. Putting Green..27

Chapter 3
Prospecting—Driving for Show and Dough...........................29
A. First Tee...29
    Sales..30
        1. Your First Call of the Day...30
        2. Cold Calling vs. Networking....................................30
        3. Always Be Closing..30
        4. You Are In Control..31
    Golf...31
        1. Preparation..31
        2. Nerves..32
B. Pre-Shot Routine..33
    Sales..33
        1. Visualize...33
        2. Assumptive..33
        3. Have Fun...33
    Golf...34
        1. Get in Your Comfort Zone......................................34
        2. Visualize...34
        3. Every Detail Must Be Consistent.............................35
C. Driving the Ball..35
    Sales..35
        1. Sales is Easier than Golf...35
        2. Different "Drives" as You Walk Through the Door......36
    Golf...36
        1. Controlled Drive...36
        2. Power Drive...37

3. Working the Ball 37
4. Know Your Limits 37
5. Alignment 38

Chapter 4
Qualifying—Eyeing the Green 39
A. Narrowing Your Focus 39
   Sales 40
      1. What are Your Qualifying Questions? 40
      2. Building a Relationship 40
   Golf 40
      1. Broad vs. Small Target 41
      2. Aggressive vs. Conservative (Decision Making) 41
      3. Scoring Opportunity 42
B. Consistency 42
   Sales 42
      1. Emotional 42
      2. Logical 43
   Golf 43
      1. Muscle Memory 43
      2. Selective Memory 44

Chapter 5
Presentations—Your Second Shot 46
A. Approach Shot 46
   Sales 47
      1. Presentation Goals 47
      2. Par-4 Sales—Two Call Close 47

3. Par-5 Sales—3+ Calls to Close 47

4. Par-3 Sales—One Call Close 47

Golf 47

1. Par-4 Strategy 48

   a. Visualize the Hole In Reverse: Green To Tee Box 48

   b. Green Light Situations 49

   c. Distance Control 49

      i. Short Irons 49

      ii. Mid To Long Irons 49

   d. 150–200 Yard Approach Shots 50

   e. 200+ Yard Approach Shots 50

   f. Par-4 Summary 50

2. Par-5 Strategy 51

   a. Plan While On The Tee Box For Second Shot 51

   b. Be Able To Adjust Your Plan 51

   c. Going For The Green 52

   d. Laying Up 52

   e. Third Shot 53

3. Par-3 Strategy 54

Chapter 6
Handling Objections—Avoiding Hazards 55

Sales 56

1. Preparation 56

2. Anticipation 56

3. Listening vs. Hearing 56

4. Build Objections into Your Sales Presentation 57

Golf...57
1. Nerves 57
2. Hazards 57
    a. Water 58
    b. Out Of Bounds 58
    c. Trees..59
    d. Bunkers 60
    e. Deep Rough..60
    f. Wind 61
3. Be Patient and Stay Focused 62

Chapter 7
Closing—Putt for Dough..63
A. Knowledge of Greens..63
    Sales 64
1. Closing the Sale—This is Why You are Here!..................64
2. Close for the Customer In Front of You..........................64
3. An Example of a Close Gone Bad....................................65
    Golf...65
1. Grass Types..65
2. Grain..66
3. Pin Locations 66
4. Green Size 66
5. Undulation..66
6. Speed..67
7. Firmness...68
8. Moisture Content..68

B. Negotiation 69
    Sales 69
    1. Give and Take...69
    2. Win/Win..69
    Golf..69
    1. Speed vs. Break..70
    2. Makeable Putts (Less than 20 Feet)...70
    3. 2-Putts (More than 20 Feet) 71

Chapter 8
Evaluation and Follow-Up—Measuring Success 72
A. Making the Cut 73
    Sales 73
    1. Sale/No Sale 73
    2. The Sale is Only Lost When … 73
    3. Making Them Your Customer for Life 73
    Golf..74
    1. Saturday 74
    2. Sunday 74
B. Playing for More than Just Money 75
    Sales 75
    1. Networking—Give Your Customer Some Business................................75
    2. Referrals—Give Yourself Some Business 75
    Golf..75
    1. Pride...75
    2. Prestige...76

C. Don't Get Ahead of Yourself 76
    Sales 77
        1. A Sale is Not a Sale Until 77
        2. Don't Spend It Before You Get It 77
    Golf 77
        1. Stay in the Moment 77
        2. Anything Can Happen Until the Last Putt Drops 77
D. Don't be a "One-Hit Wonder" 78
    Sales 78
        1. Job vs. Career 78
        2. Burnout 78
    Golf 79
        1. Follow Up/Repeat Performance 79
E. Measuring Success 79
    Sales 79
        1. Sales Par 79
        2. Sales Birdie 79
        3. Sales Eagle 79
        4. Sales Bogey 79
        5. Sales Double Bogey 80
        6. Sales Triple Bogey 80
        7. $$$$$ Earned 80
        8. $$$$$ Sold 80
        9. Units Sold 80
        10. Closing Ratio 80
        11. The Most Important Measure of Daily Success in Sales 81

Golf 81

1. Time is the True Measure...81

2. Determination..82

3. Keep Doing What Got You There and Don't Slack Off When You Become Successful. 82

Chapter 9

Keeping Score 84

Sales 84

1. Salary Plus Commission 84

2. Commission Only 85

3. Bonuses 85

4. Benefits 85

5. Perks 85

6. Travel 85

7. Awards 86

8. Contests 86

Golf 86

1. Medal (Stroke) Play 86

2. Match Play 86

3. Best Ball 88

4. Alternate Shot 88

5. Scramble 88

6. School Teams..89

7. Long Drive Contests 89

8. Practice Rounds 90

Chapter 10
The Salesperson and the Golfer—Our Story Ends 92

Postlude
A Real Life Experience 93

Appendix 95
A. My Sales/Golf Evaluation 95
B. My Summary 96
C. My Sales Scorecard 97

About the Authors 99
More Of What People Are Saying 101

Why Read This book?

If you are in sales, and we all are to some degree, you want to increase your income and/or increase your job satisfaction. If you are a golfer, you always want to legitimately lower your score and/or increase how satisfied you are with every aspect of your game. The good news is that you can increase your sales by utilizing the skills used to improve your golf game as you perform the sales cycle. Likewise, you can lower your golf score as you see how the same principles that make you a top producing sales professional can be utilized on your favorite golf course. The end result is a top producing salesperson with a golf game that is the envy of all co-workers and competitors.

To be successful in either sales or golf require the mastery of many skills. There are many books written in the business section and the sports section of your local or online bookstore that will help you fine tune your "game", no matter which genre of game it is. You are now holding in your hand two books in one.

First you have a book that covers the sales cycle as it applies to every type of sales. It does not matter if you sell products or services, the sales cycle is still the same; Preparation, Prospecting, Qualifying, Presentations, Handling Objections, Closing, and Follow-up. This book will show you the basics of each part of the sales cycle and how they relate to your ever improving golf skills.

Like wise, you have in front of you a book that discusses the skills and knowledge required to have the most well rounded golf game of anyone you know. The golf skills discussed are;

Preparation, Tee shots, Seeing the green, Approach shots, Hazards, Putting, and Evaluation of your performance. Not only will this book give you insight into each part of your game from someone who has experienced the pressure of professional tournaments, but will guide you on how to utilize this knowledge to achieve greater success as a sales professional.

Just as proficient selling and masterful golf require concentration, mastering the skills in this volume will require some of the hardest yet rewarding work of your life. Reading each section as they relate to sales and golf will require your undivided attention, but will also offer you unparalleled rewards.

Why read this book? Simply because:

Everything you need to know about sales you can learn by playing golf!!!

Sell more!!!!

Play better golf!!!!

Acknowledgements

I must acknowledge the eternal influence of Eddie Jarzabski, who allowed me to caddy for him in a tournament when I was a teenager. His dedication to, mastery of, and love for the game of golf has had a long lasting influence on me. He is thought of every time I play a round of golf.

—Peter Biadasz

I have many thanks for my esteemed list of instructors: Jack Nicklaus, Ben Hogan, Arnold Palmer, Harvey Penick, Dr. Bob Rotella, Davis Love, Jr., and Davis Love, III. Through their books, magazine articles and play on the PGA Tour, I have been able to select advice and examples that adapt well into my swing and mental approach. Using the examples of some of the finest players ever to set foot on a golf course, my golf game emerged as one that I am proud to call my own.

—Matt Eidson

Foreword

By Joe Francella—Golf Business Network

There are many books on increasing your sales and many more about lowering your golf score. To elaborate on and paraphrase a cliché, now you have the opportunity to "make 2 birdies with one golf ball."

Peter Biadasz and Matt Eidson have performed a masterful comparison between the golf process and the selling sequence. Both require practice, very specific techniques, exact thoughts for the moment, precision timing, and imaginative maneuvers for many special situations.

You've also heard it said time and again, "More big business deals are done on the golf course than anywhere else." There must be a reason behind that common reference. Trying to isolate yourself and a business associate while still at one of your offices is almost impossible. We all know this to be true. The phones are constantly ringing, there is noise from the office(s) next door, and people are rushing everywhere. Added to this are the pressures of being in the office and knowing all the business matters that require your attention right now, tomorrow and the rest of the week. These are enough to make you forget what you are trying to accomplish.

Now, picture taking that meeting outside in the sunshine and fresh air. The birds are singing. The ducks and geese are playing around the ponds. It's a totally relaxed atmosphere where you and your business associate will spend the next four to five hours riding together in a golf cart.

Today, golf is the fastest growing sport in America. It is evident that there must be a good reason for that. Can the setting be any more perfect? It will be so easy to get to know your client better in such a serene setting. Most business deals, especially deals created by someone selling his products or ideas, in my experience are generated from a composite built between the seller and the buyer. I have yet to see a faster composite built between buyer and seller than one built on the golf course. Plus, there are the never ending discussions about the finer points of golf, regardless of who is the better golfer.

People are always looking to deal with the best people available when they buy products and services—that's just human nature. Good golfers are presumed to be the best in their fields and they automatically earn respect from the buyers. Golfers know what it takes to become an accomplished golfer! That should be reason enough to buy this book.

So, become a better golfer by practicing the comparisons between golf and selling. Learn how to make yourself a better salesperson by learning the success principles utilized in becoming a better golfer.

Introduction

You Need This Book If ...

- You are a sales professional and want to increase your sales and improve your income.
- You are a golfer of any level desiring to improve your golf game and lower your score.
- You want more information to see if sales is a career option for you.
- You have heard that golf is a great sport but know nothing about it.
- You are a sales manager and want to combine the advantages of sales with the recreation of golf.
- You are in sales and feel that you have reached a frustrating plateau.
- You just want to have fun playing golf.

How This Book is Organized:

Chapter 1 takes you on a journey of how the salesperson and the golfer discovered that everything you need to know about sales you can learn by playing golf.

Chapter 2 shows you how to prepare for the best day of sales or best round of golf you have ever experienced.

Chapter 3 discusses how prospecting for new clients is the same as driving the ball.

Chapter 4 shows you how to eye the *green* by qualifying your prospect and your golf shot.

Chapter 5 teaches appropriate strategy for your presentations and your approach shot as you get closer to your goal.

Chapter 6 discusses the objections and hazards that we may encounter.

Chapter 7 talks about closing the sale and putting the ball in the cup.

Chapter 8 offers perspective on measuring your success, as well as follow-up.

Chapter 9 lets you explore the many formats of sales and golf.

Chapter 10 concludes as to how to best utilize your newly learned knowledge.

Postlude will bring a smile to your face.

How To Use This Book

Each chapter discusses the topics at hand, first as they relate to sales, then in terms of golf. The "Concept" section at the beginning of each chapter gives you the mindset of the chapter as you relate sales and golf together. The "Practical Applications" at the end of each chapter will help you live what had been discussed in the chapter. As you read the material, make note of your strong points as well as your weaknesses.

At the end of every chapter you will have the opportunity to list the one item in that chapter on which you will focus to increase your sales production as well as lower your golf score. By the end of the book you will have listed items that will improve your mastery of every aspect of the sales cycle as well as identify and resolve the weaknesses in your golf game. You can record the item that you have listed at the end of each chapter in Appendix II.

As you go about your sales day, realize the parallels between your successes in golf to increasing one's sales. As you play each round of golf, realize that the key to lowering your score can be found in mastering every aspect of the sales cycle.

For example, the next time you are prospecting, relate it to driving the ball off of the tee. During your next critical putt, remember that you are closing the sale. The parallels are there for every aspect of the sales cycle as well as your golf game. This book will assist you in this discovery.

Enjoy the book. Increase your sales ... and lower your golf score!!!

Chapter 1

The Salesperson and the Golfer—Our Story Begins

This is a true story:

At a holiday cookout a professional salesperson and a professional golfer continued a discussion they had been having for a month. The salesperson, wanting to be a better golfer (he was a very bad golfer at this point in time, being very new to the game as a serious player) was asking many good, and a few stupid, questions of the golfer in an attempt to improve his game. The golfer, with a wealth of knowledge, was sharing some amazing information with the salesperson.

In the meantime, the golfer, looking to branch out into the business world, was asking the salesperson for some much needed advice and information. The salesperson, never at a loss for words, freely shared his years of sales experience.

After some very lively and informative discussion, both the salesperson and the golfer realized that while they were talking the vocabulary of sales and golf, they were discussing the same principles of success. They had the same ideas but different languages.

Both discussed the importance of preparation. But the salesperson also talked about prospecting, qualifying, presenting, handling objections, closing, and follow-up. This is known as the sales cycle. In the meantime, the golfer detailed driving the ball off the tee, looking at the green, approach shot strategy, dealing with hazards, putting and evaluation of ones game. This is known as good, consistent golf. Each sales topic directly relates to a golf topic:

Preparation/Preparation
Prospecting/Tee shot
Qualifying/See the green
Presentations/Approach shot
Handling Objections/Hazards
Closing/Putting
Follow-up/Evaluation

To be specific, the thoughts and ideas discussed over time to improve ones sales and lower ones golf score were ...

Chapter 2

Preparation—The Making of a Professional

CONCEPT (Tying sales and golf together): Whether you want to be a successful salesperson or an accomplished golfer, it is imperative that you determine your level of dedication up front. Set some goals and then develop and implement a plan that will help you realize them. Be realistic and honest with yourself and then make it happen through effective use of your time.

The road to success is less frustrating if you truly learn to love the process of improving and honing your skills. Be careful of how you treat co-workers and fellow golfers on the way up or else you will be doomed to see them again on your way down the ladder. Proper manners go a long way in business and on the golf course. Know the rules and always abide by them.

Educate yourself about your business and about the game of golf. In either venture, ignorance is not bliss. Make the most of the tools that you will use to get the job done. Refine them as needed. You have to know your industry and your competition to be an effective salesperson, and you must know the course you're playing in golf and who you are up against.

Lastly, never enter the battle without proper preparation. Take care of yourself physically and mentally, and always go through your routine before visiting a potential client or the first tee box.

There is no such thing as an overnight success. To be the best takes preparation. Often this preparation is seen only by the one doing the preparing. Do you think that the best sales people are born as the best? Do you believe that the world's greatest golfers entered this world with incredible talent that was already matured? For every success you observe, know that an enormous amount of preparation paved the way. This is how you prepare as a professional.

A. Determine Your Level of Dedication

To be good at anything you have to take the time to educate yourself as well as acquire and refine the specific skills necessary to become successful. This is especially true for selling and golf. You may tell others you want to be great at something, but what you tell yourself truly determines your heartfelt level of dedication to the task at hand.

<u>Sales</u>

1. Life Goals

What are your personal and professional goals for the next year? Five years? Ten years? Twenty years? Are your personal and professional goals compatible with each other? What are you willing to do to attain and achieve those goals? What types of skills and what knowledge will you need to acquire, refine and master to reach each goal?

Sounds like a lot? It is!!! But it is your life and ultimately you are the one responsible for you, your successes, and non-successes. (How is that for a positive perspective?) There are many great goal planning tools available to you. They can be found on the internet, in bookstores, or in your local library. The best goal planning, not only takes a thorough look at every aspect of your life, but also combines time lines and step by step activities to ensure your goals are achieved timely and efficiently. Whichever goal planning tool you utilize, be sure to examine the following areas of your life:

- Both your personal and professional sides of life
- Your spiritual life
- Your physical well being
- Your personality and character traits
- Your assets and liabilities (financially, personally and professionally)
- Your contributions to those around you and society in general
- Your income

2. Income

If you are in sales, you will hear your co-workers, your manager and maybe yourself say, "I am going to make a six figure income!!!" It gets interesting when you ask these people how they are going to achieve that goal. Many times they do not even know how many sales a month they need to close to achieve that income. Or worse yet, how many calls a day they must make to get to their publicly stated goal. Whatever income you decide you want to attain, be sure to understand the work and dedication it takes to earn those dollars.

Specifically, when you decide what you want your income to realistically be, based on your expenditures and saving habits, figure how much you must earn each month, day, and hour to know how your goal affects your work routine. Keep track of how many calls you have to make to find a true prospect, how many prospects you have to have to make a sale, and how much income you achieve from each sale. You can then figure how many calls you have to make each day or hour to achieve your desired income.

For example, let's say I want to earn $50,000 a year. With fifty work weeks in a year (leave out two weeks for vacation and personal time) that means I must earn $1,000.00 per week or $200.00 per day to reach my stated goal. If I have to make five calls to find one prospect, I close 33% of my prospects, and I make $100.00 per sale then I must make 30 calls each day to achieve my goal of two sales a day. In other words, I must make two sales a day to earn $200.00, which means I present to six prospects (closing ratio of 33%), and to find those six prospects I had to make 30 calls, five for each prospect found.

Based on how long your work day is, you can calculate how many calls you need to make every hour. Of course, your goal is to become more efficient in every step of the sales cycle so that you can either make fewer calls to achieve your desired income, or make the same number of calls and achieve higher income. The information in this book will assist you in getting to the point of having to make that decision. We will discuss this more in chapter 8.

Golf

1. What Is Your Level Of Dedication?

The first areas of preparation occur long before you ever reach the golf course. Before you even bother going to the golf course again, you need to decide what type of golfer you want to be or, in other words, what you want to achieve by playing golf and what you expect to get back out of it. I tell my friends this all the time. They want to play better golf but they aren't willing to put in the time and effort it takes to achieve better golf when I explain to them what it entails. Be realistic with yourself and figure out how determined you are and how important it is to you to improve your golf game. If you just want to shave a few strokes off your average score to make the game more enjoyable, then most golfers can achieve that goal in a short period of time simply by learning better course management. However, if you truly want to be the absolute best golfer that you are capable of being (granted: this does not mean making it to the PGA Tour), then become a student of the game, dedicate time to practice every week, and make it a priority in your life.

2. Be The Best You Can Be

Many of you might be thinking to yourself: "But I'm already a golf addict and my spouse complains about how much time I'm playing now, much less adding more time!" Well, it may not be that you need to add more time ... just more effective use of that time. Practicing the wrong thing doesn't count as time dedicated to improvement. In fact, it's simply a waste of time. Comparatively, too much playing golf and not enough practice can be detrimental, too, because when we're on the golf course we tend to fix our swing problems with little adjustments, or band-aids, to get us through the round but ultimately make our problems worse. Harvey Penick used to tell his students "play with the swing you brought." This means that if you normally play a fade and then go to the course one day and find yourself with a bad slice, don't start trying to work out the kinks while you're playing, just aim farther left and allow for the slice. When you get done, go to the range and work it out. Don't play again, if possible, until you have it worked out at the range. [If you were on a sales call and were asked a question about your product or service that you didn't know the answer to, would you go out on another sales call without first learning the answer?] Obviously, this is not how the purely recreational golfer would deal with the problem, but this book was not developed for that golfer; instead, this book is intended to help the golfer that is dedicated to improvement and playing the best golf that he/she is physically capable of achieving.

B. Effective Use Of Practice Time/Become A Student Of The Game

Did you know that what you don't know can cost you in many ways? In sales it will cost you $$$$$$ in lost sales. When golfing, it will cost you strokes. This may translate into the difference between winning and losing, no matter in which endeavor you are participating.

<u>Sales</u>

1. Lack of Knowledge Will Cost You $$$$$

As with any profession, the more you know, the more professional and proficient you will be. Have you ever "known" you were going to make a sale only to lose to another sales professional. Maybe you were left scratching your head asking "how did I lose that sale? I know I had it won." When you start adding up the lost dollars it may make you sick, and that is just on the lost sales you know about. Many sales professionals are very good at creating a sale when there is not an obvious need. It is through their expertise of every aspect of the sales cycle that they are proficient at communicating how their product or service can benefit a prospect, even when the prospect does not even know they have a need.

2. Practice Every Part of the Sales Cycle

When you are watching golf on television and you see both spectacular and ordinary shot, do you know how many hundreds, if not thousands of balls were hit by that professional to achieve the desired results? It is the same in sales. Over the years, your rear-view car mirror should hear both your spectacular and non-spectacular prospecting opening lines, your qualifying questions, presentations galore, answers to objections, closing statements and follow-up demeanor. The first time you make a statement to a prospect or customer should not be the first time the statement comes out of your mouth.

Practice, practice, practice. Then practice some more. Role play with co-workers, family members, and friends. Get constructive feedback on your mastery of the sales cycle. Learn from the good and bad examples of others, as they learn from you. Also, when you buy products or services for yourself, critique the salesperson attempting to sell you their product or service. You may see a part of the sales cycle presented in a new or unique way. You may also learn from others mistakes.

The greatest thing about the sales cycle is that the cycle is the same no matter what you sell, and always in the same order. Depending on what you sell some parts of the cycle may be longer or shorter. But it is still the sales cycle.

Golf

1. Make Sure You Practice the Right Things

How do you become a student of the game? You can, literally, become a student by hiring a golf professional to give you lessons but, not to discourage that by any means, you can learn a lot on your own by reading books, watching videos, studying the history of golf and the various philosophical approaches to the game, and by watching the world's best players on television.

The important thing to clarify is that you should not get locked into just one school of thought. Study all that is available and then make an educated decision as to which theories will work for you by trying them out and giving each one a legitimate amount of effort. Once you have determined what feels comfortable for you then you can set some goals, track your improvement and play with the confidence that comes from knowing that you have made an educated attempt at becoming a better golfer.

I (Matt) believe that it is also important to know some golf history. Even if history is not your thing, anyone can benefit from knowing where the game has been and how it got to be what it is today. It has been said that, in life, you cannot know where you're going if you don't know where you've been. The same is true in golf.

2. Be Dedicated to Improvement

There is no point in studying the game of golf and searching out the various theories if you do not wholly dedicate yourself to the process of improvement. That means that you will probably have to accept the fact that you will get worse before you get better. The best approach is to learn to enjoy the process of gradual improvement. Don't expect to stumble upon some magical solution that will fix your golf swing overnight. Anything worth doing is going to take time, so accept it, enjoy the process and do not falter in your dedication.

C. Etiquette

Every game has rules both written and unwritten. By knowing these principles you will find your experiences to be much more enjoyable. Yes, you may be in the field of battle but you are also on the field of play.

Sales

1. How You Treat Yourself

You will never treat anyone else better than you treat yourself. Don't get stuck on yourself to the exclusion of others, just treat yourself right. Many times this is nothing more than getting the right amount of sleep, proper diet, and appropriate exercise. It also means having a good support group with family and friends. Balance in every part of your life is important. Many times you can trace stress or other negative things in your life to being out of balance in each of these areas. Treat yourself right and you will have a solid frame of reference on which to treat others.

2. How You Treat Others

The most important way in which you treat others can be summed up in one word—sincere. In the world of sales there is a lot of insincerity disguised as 'please buy my product or service.' Treat others as you want to be treated. Mary Kay Ash summed it in this way, "Every time I meet someone I pretend they have a sign on them that says *I AM IMPORTANT.*". As a sales person, you may always get someone to buy from you once. A successful sales professional will always get someone to buy from him again and again, even when the price may be lower somewhere else. Customers know value, and they know you, and how you treat your prospects/customers are a part of that value.

Golf

The first step is learning the proper etiquette. Golf is a gentleman's game and its procedures, rules, and etiquette definitely fall into the category of "what you don't know ***will*** hurt you." Unfortunately, proper etiquette is most easily learned while playing the game. You will, inevitably, embarrass yourself someday on the golf course by not knowing some of the intricacies of acceptable behavior, and probably more than once. Nonetheless, there are books that you can read to help you avoid most embarrassing situations and I highly recommend finding a mentor (parent, older sibling, coach or friend) that has played for a number of years and is willing to help you without humiliating you.

1. Keep Up a Good Pace of Play

The simplest thing to do, though, is just to make sure that you keep up a good pace. I have never minded playing with someone who is well on their way to 115 strokes just so long as they are keeping up an acceptable pace. At that level of golf, it is not necessary to study every putt from four different angles, pace off yardages from the 150 for 30 yards, take a mulligan on every hole, or look for every lost ball for a full five minutes. Be courteous to your fellow players and those behind you; play as quickly as possible until you improve enough to validate taking more time on each shot. I don't mind bad golfers and I don't mind slow golfers; but nobody can stand a slow bad golfer.

2. Proper Manners on the Tee Box, In the Fairway, On the Green, and In the Clubhouse

Other important areas of etiquette include proper manners on the tee box, in the fairway, around the green, and even in the clubhouse. Let's address each one briefly, starting with the tee box. In tournament situations the starter will assign an order for each foursome. In casual play, be courteous and always offer the box to your playing partners first. Always maintain silence while someone is addressing the ball, during their swing and, when possible, try not to stand directly behind their swing path where they might be distracted by you during their swing. The optimal place to stand is several yards behind the golfer's backside. Also, make sure your shadow is not intruding on their stance or near the ball, as this can be very distracting with even a slight movement. Try to keep an eye on their ball in case they need help finding it and always try to find something positive to say about their shot or say nothing at all. I understand that good friends will want to rib each other but I am speaking of competitive situations or cases where you are not close enough with your playing partners to kid around. After play begins, remember the honor system. Starting with the second tee, the player with the best score on the previous hole has the *honor* and should be allowed to play first, unless they offer to let someone else who is ready in order to keep a proper pace of play, commonly referred to as "ready" golf.

Once you have reached the fairway, rough, or wherever your second shots are to be played from, the person farthest from the hole always has the honor. It is important not to walk ahead of them, as this can be very nerve wracking for golfers of limited ability because they are afraid they might hit a poor shot and hit you. Better golfers walk slightly ahead of each other all the time because the likelihood of a "shanked" shot is so minimal that it is not a concern, but please be courteous if you are playing with mid to high handicappers that are not as confident. Again, keep an eye on your playing partner's shots to assist in finding the ball if it becomes lost.

When your group has reached the green, the same rule applies with regard to honor. So, be sure to let the person farthest from the hole play first. If that person is you and you are on the green but one of your partners is not, even though they are closer to the hole, it is proper etiquette to allow them to play first, especially if they are chipping or playing from a bunker. If everyone in the group has missed the green with their approach shots and one of the players is in a bunker, allow that person to play first because it will take them longer to get prepared to putt because they will have to rake the bunker.

While etiquette on the tee box and in the fairway is very important, exercising proper behavior around the green is the most important because there are so many intricacies. On the top of the list is being careful not to walk on another player's line. According to the USGA, a golfer's putting line is defined as "*the line that the player wishes his ball to take after a* stroke *on the* putting green. Except with respect to Rule 16-1e, the line of putt *includes a reasonable distance on either side of the intended line. The* line of putt *does not extend beyond the* hole." While it is important to note that a player whose ball is not on the putting surface does not officially have a line of putt yet, it is still good manners not to walk across the line of someone who is on the apron or within a few feet of the putting surface, even if they are chipping. Also, the biggest reason that walking on someone's line is such a faux pas is because of the possible damage that can be done to the surface if you drag your feet. Therefore, pick up your feet at all times when walking on the green so that you do not create any spike marks that someone may have to putt through, even if it may be a player in one of the groups behind you.

The next area of concern is tending the pin. In my experience, if you are not a professional, scratch amateur, or have no caddie experience then you probably are not tending the flagstick correctly. As noted above, being mindful of other players' lines is priority number one. Next, be sure to stand on the side of the hole where you will not be casting a shadow over the hole or the player's putting line.

When grabbing the pin, get a hold of the flag first and wrap it around the stick so it doesn't flap in the wind creating a distracting noise. Remove the flagstick from the cup and then replace it without actually inserting the base back into the hole at the bottom of the cup. Carefully place the base of the flagstick on the inside rim and lean the pin backward (or towards yourself.) This procedure eliminates the possibility of yanking the pin out and lifting the cup above ground level while the ball is rolling towards it, effectively blocking the putt. Don't think that scenario sounds likely to happen? Think again. It happens more often than you think.

The final aspect of etiquette is often overlooked because it refers to your behavior in the clubhouse or locker room and not on the course. Remember, once again, that golf is a gentleman's game; therefore, it is fine to be proud of a great shot or a great round but take care not to offend golfers of less caliber by boasting or "rubbing it in." Be humble and you will discover that your story will circulate without your assistance. In contrast, if you are not such a good golfer and happen to play a surprisingly good round of golf, or a particularly great shot, be aware that the better players in the clubhouse are not really going to be impressed with your performance. They will be happy for you and will congratulate you so long as you don't go overboard. Regardless of the accomplishment, let others tell the story for you, unless someone asks you about it because golfers are like fishermen: they love to tell stories.

D. Equipment

Both sales and golf have equipment that is vital to ensure you are playing at the very highest level of your game. Acquire the best and use it wisely.

<u>Sales</u>

1. Your Brain (Attitude—Your Most Important Asset)

Wouldn't you agree that a person with a great attitude and mediocre competence would always be more successful than a person with a horrible attitude and good competence? Have you ever known someone with a bad attitude? When they called you or approached you in public, didn't you find a creative way to avoid talking with them? What happens when you call someone? Can you picture them diving over a desk to get to the phone because *you* are calling them? Or are they intentionally sending the call to voicemail?

Would you be more likely to do business with someone with a good attitude or a bad attitude? If you are like me, you do business with those people that will treat the customer the same way that you do.

Understanding that attitude is the most important asset that you have as a salesperson. Here are some things you can do to help maintain a positive attitude.

When the alarm clock makes that unpleasant sound in the morning, *make the decision* that you are going to be positive. Any decision made enough times becomes a habit. Being positive can be as much a habit as being negative. When my alarm clock screams at me I just start praying. That usually helps my decision.

You can't put a smile on someone else's face unless you have a smile on yours so … *put a smile on someone's face by 9:00 a.m. everyday*. This can be the most fun for you and the most frustrating for those around you.

Peter once had a boss that just hated it when he would stop by her office every morning to say a very cheery "good morning." However, two weeks after Peter left for a better position, he received a call from her letting me know that not only did she really appreciate the thought every morning but that her day was not the same because no one else was saying "good morning." You never know what kind of "seeds" you are planting.

You do not have to have the title of manager to be the *mood manager* of your company. Set the example and standard of what a positive attitude is at your place of business, at home, and everywhere you go. You may be surprised how many people you can influence in this manner.

Anticipate problems before they happen. When was the last time a truly *new* problem presented itself, one that you had never been exposed to directly or indirectly through your own or someone else's experience? Let's face it; so many times we get upset over the same thing. It's time to develop a new habit!

Give *sincere compliments* on an hourly basis. Sincere is the key word. People will know if you are not being real in what you are expressing. Also, by complimenting others, you are looking for the good in them.

Finally, *develop points of reference*. When you are going through a truly rough time, you can think in one of two directions: A) think about the best time of your life or something that makes you laugh as an escape or B) think about the worst time in your life and realize that you made it through that bad event so you can make it through this bad event.

Always remember that your attitude is your most important asset.

2. Your Education

Many people think that their education stops when they receive their diploma. Actually, that is when the education begins. If done properly, the education ends when they pronounce you as deceased. On-going education can take many forms, such as:

- Formal classes
- On-line training
- Books or other reading materials
- CD's of related material
- Mentors
- Seminars
- Fill in the blank_____

Ensure that you learn something new everyday of your life. Then, and only then, will you find yourself with the elite of your profession.

3. Your Appearance

First impressions are very important. Before a word comes out of your mouth, many times people have already made some sort of decision about you. In fact, you may find yourself doing this from time to time.

Sales professionals dress appropriate for their industry, locale, and customer base. Be well groomed. And remember, all sales professional have a pen with them. You never know when someone may need one to sign your paperwork. It is amazing how many salespeople do not have a writing instrument with them at all times.

4. Your "Sales Ball"

Your "sales ball" is the sales process—the sales cycle. As you go through the sales cycle from this day forward imagine that you have placed your "sales ball" on the tee, hit it in the fairway, placed it on the green, and closed the sale by putting into the cup. You may occasionally hit it into a hazard, but you are a professional at handling objections and keeping the ball in play. While your "sales ball" may be imaginary, it will guide you to perfect your sales game.

5. The Inner Game Of Sales

a. Self Motivation

There are two types of motivation: internal and external. External motivation relies on other people and things to ensure a high level of productivity. This is usually short lived and relies constantly on new stimuli to keep the process active. Internal motivation comes from within and is guided by the realization, implementation, and execution of goals, both personal and professional. Every successful salesperson treats their sales "job" as if they own their own company, with appropriate goals for success with this company. Making this perceived self owned company successful is a driving source of this internal motivation. Internal motivation is constant and stronger than any external motivation that can be exerted. This mindset means that these successful salespeople feel as though they have the support of a great company behind them to take care of service, administration, billing, parts, etc. to support their high sales activity level. While feeling they are more than just employees, they flourish in an environment of success they create. Self motivated salespeople are the easiest to manage because they are self managed. They are the easiest to train because they are eager to learn. Be warned, self motivated salespeople are a nightmare to manage if the sales manager wants to be a controlling, adult babysitter. Yet these professionals will be successful in spite of their manager, or will move onto an environment where they will flourish.

b. Independence

The self motivated are truly independent because they know what to do and they do it. They do not need someone hanging over their shoulder to get the work done. Some sales managers attempt to justify their position by becoming the aforementioned controlling, adult babysitter. I (Peter) have always felt that a sales manager justifies him or herself only by producing high numbers of quality sales. Understanding this, when I became district sales manager for a company, the first thing I did was cancel all of the sales meetings. The sales team exclaimed, "How can we sell without at least weekly sales meetings?" I explained to them that they were a team of self motivated, independent sales professionals and that I was not going to buy from them, and therefore asked, "Why would they want to be in front of me instead of live prospects?"

The result was such an increase in productivity, sales numbers, and attitude we became the number one office for the company for quite a long time. We did one-on-one training as needed, communicated a lot by phone, e-mail, and had a *short* monthly meeting as a group so we could ensure we were all on the same page. Not only were we the top sales office in the company, but had the lowest employee turnover rate of any department in the entire company. By getting out of the way and letting my sales people do what they do best, the sales cycle, I was looked upon as a master sales manager. The truth was we had a great team from top to bottom. The best collection of people one could hire. I felt honored for being associated with this finest of sales teams.

c. Professionalism

There are many attributes and qualities to being a professional. However, professionalism is a state of mind that ensures that trying to being a professional does not come across as a bad acting attempt. Professionalism involves knowing you are on your way to being the best because everyday you are studying the materials or learning from mentors to be excellent both professionally and personally. It also means being sincere and truly treating others as you want to be treated, while improving in this area daily. Professionalism comes from within. Being a true professional is the external manifestation of the qualities of professionalism.

Golf

1. Custom Fitting

Custom fitting is a process by which a golf professional, or a professional clubmaker, watches you hit a number of balls with a 5 or 6-iron, and then a driver, and then analyzes the statistical information collected. This is done in order to provide each individual with a set of clubs that fit him/her, specifically, from the club head to the shaft and the grips. The information collected and analyzed will range from body measurements, such as height and wrist-to-floor length, to swing speed, shaft length, flex and torque, offset, swing weight, total weight, optimal trajectory and launch angle, load, grip type and size, and lie angle. A professional golfer will, obviously, see more benefit from custom fitting because their game is so fine tuned that every little detail translates into strokes lost or gained, and that means big money, nowadays. However, every golfer will benefit to some degree from having their clubs custom fitted for him. We all have very different bodies and swing types, so why would you expect to walk into a store and buy a set of clubs "off the rack" that fit you perfectly? The game is hard enough ... don't make it harder by playing with equipment that isn't right for you. Besides, by going through the custom fitting process, you will become much more educated about golf equipment and your own swing. There's a lot to be said for the confident feeling that you get when you stand over a golf club that you know is built to fit your game.

2. Choosing the Right Woods, Irons, Wedges, Putter, Golf Ball and Tee

After you have been through the custom fitting process and have a good understanding of the equipment that will best suit your game, then it is time to research the woods, irons, wedges, putters and golf balls that are on the market and find the right ones for you. Starting with the driver, the first decision is whether you want to find a club that will help add a few yards or one that will be easy for you to control. If you're lucky, you can get one that will do both, but that is not very common, unfortunately. Of course, every manufacturer claims that their driver will provide the longest and straightest drivers of your life, but be smart and buy the one that is right for you and not the driver that has the best advertising campaign. When choosing your fairway woods or hybrid clubs, you will also want to consider your goals before making a purchase. For instance, do you want to have a 3-wood that is your "old reliable" club off the tee when you have to hit a fairway? Or, do you want one that you can hit higher and longer so that you can go for par-5's on your second shot even if it's a long, forced carry? Again, it's possible to find one that is both consistent and long, but you need to decide which is more important to you. Then do your shopping accordingly.

When it comes to choosing your irons, this decision needs a lot of thought and careful research, including hitting as many demo irons as you can find. Most of your strokes during a round of golf will come from the use of your irons (3-PW), so choose wisely. The first choice in iron selection is whether to go with scoring irons or game improvement clubs. In other words, do you want irons that allow you to work the ball both directions (draw or fade,) thus providing the ability to be more creative on the golf course? Or, do you prefer to simply hit the ball as straight as possible? There is no right or wrong choice from a golf perspective, only from your own personal point of view. Choose the irons that will help *you* accomplish what *you* want to on the golf course. If you enjoy being a creative shot maker, then look at buying some blades or any type of iron that has more weight centered in the middle of the club and not around the perimeter. If simplicity fits your game better, then shop the game improvement irons that provide perimeter weighting and a low, deep center of gravity that will help get the ball up quickly and provide more forgiveness. Your choice of irons should reflect your mental approach to the game.

I will relate this personal story that I experienced early in my amateur career that enlightened me to the importance of choosing the right irons. When I was an 18-handicapper, I purchased a set of oversized, cast-iron, game improvement irons complete with perimeter weighting, cavity back, and plenty of offset. They were very forgiving and I gained some distance but, since my natural shot is a right-to-left draw, the offset was causing me to hook the ball and miss a lot of shots to the left. Also, the perimeter weighting made it near impossible to work the ball or control the trajectory. Using these irons, I was able to shave my handicap down to a 7 but then I got stuck there and couldn't seem to improve anymore. It was at this point that I decided to go for my first real custom fitting session, wherein I learned that these irons were all wrong for me and my game. I was fitted with a set of forged blades with very little offset and most of the weight in the center of the club. These irons allowed me to hit a soft draw instead of the hook, and they gave me the ability to control my trajectory at will, including working the ball both directions and hitting the ball high or low when needed. After stagnating at the 7-handicap level for quite some time, I was down to a 2-handicap within three months and then turned pro about a year later. This is what worked for me and I encourage you to actively seek out what works for you. Do not be afraid to experiment and fail because eventually you will find the right equipment that will allow you to maximize your potential.

With regard to your wedges (gap, sand, and lob) there is a lot more "feel" to consider than your other irons. Wedges are your scoring irons, so you need to find some that feel good in your hands, have the right amount of bounce, and give you enough confidence to go pin-hunting when you have the chance. First, be sure to get wedges that separate your lofts evenly so that you can be consistent with your swing. For example, standard pitching wedges have 46–48 degrees of loft so, if yours has 46 degrees, then your next wedges should be 52 and 58 degrees so that you have 6 degrees between each club. If your pitching wedge has 48 degrees of loft, then look for 54 and 60 degree wedges to complement the set. This theory may not work for everyone, but you should have some sort of plan when buying wedges. Also, if you live in an area of the country where the ground is usually firm, then you need to choose wedges with less bounce to avoid hitting too many "skulled" shots. If you live in a wet area of the country and the courses you play are typically soft, too little bounce will cause you to hit a lot of "fat" shots. Again, the only way to find the wedges that will be perfect for you requires a lot of experimentation, so it may take some time but it will be worth it in the end because having confidence in your wedges is essential to shooting low scores.

When it comes to "feel," there is no more important club purchase than your putter. Since "feel" is the most important factor in selecting the best putter for you, it is also the most difficult factor in the buying equation. There has probably never been a player in history that owns more putters than Arnold Palmer. Arnold was always a "feel" player, though, so he changed his putter constantly, according to how it felt on that particular day. While I do not recommend changing putters every time you play, it is not a bad idea to own at least three or four so that you can change when needed. Sometimes just standing over something different can help you focus more and erase the bad memories of several missed putts. Also, if you are not confident with your chipping, consider getting a mallet putter that is easier to use from the off the green. Mallets are heavier and are less likely to get caught up in the grass when putting from the fringe. If you putt cross-handed, then you should find a putter with some offset to reduce your chances of pulling putts to the inside. Whatever the case might be, do plenty of experimenting and when you find a putter that gives you confidence, keep it because that's the most important thing to have when you're standing over a five-footer to win a tournament.

The last decision to make is which golf ball to play. Save this choice for last because it should have a lot to do with your previous equipment decisions. For instance, if you have decided to buy a set of blades so that you can hit cuts and draws, at will, then you should also choose a ball that offers more spin because you will need spin to be able to work the ball around the course. If straight and consistent is what you're after, then play a reduced spin golf ball that is less likely to get off line. If you are a short game fanatic, then you will also want a softer ball with a higher spin rate. The most important factor is to always play the same golf ball. If you are going to be serious about your game, do not play with golf balls that you found in the water or the woods. You can collect them, if you wish, but use them as shag balls or only in scrambles when you want to take risky tee shots. To become completely familiar with your own game, you must play the same golf ball all the time so that you know exactly how it will react in all situations and conditions. Maintaining consistency is the most important thing that you can do for yourself when making decisions about your equipment.

One footnote when thinking about your equipment is to be sure and use the type of tee that will best suit your driver and ball choices. With the size of modern driver heads, you will most likely want to get some longer tees so you can tee the ball higher. If you tee it too low and you're playing with a 400cc driver, you are not giving yourself much of a chance to catch the sweet spot on the driver face. In addition, when it comes to par 3's, always use a tee, even if it's just a broken one that you find on the tee box. Sam Snead once said that he never met a golfer that was so good that he couldn't use a perfect lie when it was available [from *Every Shot I Take* by Davis Love III]. So, do not get cocky and throw your ball down on the ground and hit it because you think you're so good that you don't need a tee on par 3's.

3. Care and Maintenance

Once you have a bag full of equipment that fits your game perfectly, the next step is to make sure that you maintain your clubs properly. Keep your clubs clean as often as possible. If you play at least 5–10 times per month, then you should re-grip your clubs every year. If you are playing with soft, forged irons then be sure to have the loft and lie angles checked every three months. Your short irons, especially, will bend as you play with them because of the sharper, more descending angle as you hit the into the ground after the ball. Cast irons are less likely to bend, but they will through time. I suggest having them checked at least twice a year if you play regularly. If you play with graphite shafts in your irons, then you will want to have the set re-shafted every two to five years depending upon how often you play and the quality of the shaft. Graphite deteriorates quicker than steel, so if you start losing distance with your irons or find yourself hitting some wild shots then your shafts may be the problem. Graphite usually deteriorates on the inside so it may not even be visible, but you might have a serious loss of quality in the shafts.

4. Different Equipment for Different Courses or Conditions

The prepared professional will carry extra clubs to each event knowing that this week's course may require some different shots than last week's venue. So, you must learn to prepare for particular courses and, more specifically, particular holes. For instance, some courses require a lot of forced carries over sand or water to the greens. Therefore, it may be appropriate to pull out your low-hitting 2-iron and 3-iron then replace them with a higher launching 5-wood and 7-wood, respectively. Hybrid clubs are popular long iron replacements, as well. In contrast, other courses may allow for run-up shots to the greens and you will want to keep the long irons in the bag for better trajectory control and workability. Playing in windy conditions such as Hawaii or west Texas may encourage you to use a driver with less loft and lower torque in the shaft for a lower, uncontrolled trajectory. The same might be said for hard, dry conditions where you want a lot of roll on your tee shots. Playing in the northeast part of the U.S., however, may compel you to use a driver with more loft and a softer shaft to maximize your carry distance in softer ground conditions. Pros will also change wedges according to the ground and/or sand conditions, and putters according to the speed or grain of the greens. The important thing is to be prepared to adapt to different conditions at each venue.

E. Knowledge of the Course

Knowledge is power. The more knowledge you have, the better your odds of making that sale and lowering your golf score. Knowing how to identify what is good, valid and useful information is important. This way we are not filled with useless and unnecessary trivia that will get in the way of our most important goal.

Sales

1. Your Product/Service/Company

Make it a goal to know more about your product or service than anyone in your company. This does not mean just facts and specification, but also the benefits of what you sell and how that translates into practical applications for your prospect, soon to be customer.

Also, learn as much as you can about those that service your customer after the sale. A great product with bad service will mean no repeat business or referrals for you.

Finally, learn as much about your company as you can. Not just its history, but why it is the best at what it does. Learn how to tell the story of your company in such a compelling and convincing fashion that everyone you tell it to will want to be associated with it. That way, they become a part of the story of your company's success.

2. Your Industry

After you have mastered knowledge of your product/service and company, become a student of your industry. It is very helpful to know history, trends, strong points, and weaknesses. Make it your goal to become the industry expert. As such, you will have the greatest advantage over your competitors.

3. Your Target Market/Prospects

Knowing your target market is big picture knowledge. In narrowing your focus, you get to know your prospect. There are target markets and prospects that are more profitable than others. Identify them. Some are easier to close and some are trouble. By researching, you actually are utilizing what will become a time management tool for you. Also, this knowledge will enable you to better personalize these relationships.

4. Your Competition

Know your competition better than they know you. Learn about their products/services, history, strengths, weaknesses, financials, key employees, trends, practices, and anything else you can think of. Talk with their customers. You can never obtain enough information about your competitors. However, make sure you only utilize means which are legal, moral and ethical.

There have been times I (Peter) have visited my competitors. I have always been amazed at how much information a competitor will give away. One time, while visiting a competitor's showroom I was allowed to use one of their telephones, which I promptly utilized to close a sale. One more sale for me, one less sale for them.

Another time I brought a sales representative with me that I was training. He was quite nervous about being in "enemy territory." After being greeted by a competitor sales rep, given a tour of the show room and receiving much information we went on our way. Upon getting into my car I turned to my rep and asked him what one thing the competitor did not ask of us. After quite a while of not being able to answer the question I became more than just a little upset with my rep. You see, our competitor never asked us who we were or who we were with. The competition had just given a great demonstration of who they were, what they could do, and how much they would charge, but had no way to follow up with us to get the sale. I wonder how many sales they had lost over the years due to this practice. I assure you from that day forward we always knew who we were talking with and how to follow-up with the prospect.

You can learn much from competitors; how to do the job right, and how to do the job wrong.

Golf

1. Course Rating and Slope Rating

Upon arriving at the course, first acquire a scorecard and a yardage book, if available. Study the layout, yardages, course rating, and the slope ratings. The well-prepared pro will know how course and slope ratings are calculated, for it gives you the ability to get an overall feel for the difficulty of the course before ever seeing it. Course ratings are, essentially, what a scratch golfer would be expected to shoot from the particular tee box being rated. The USGA has a formula for calculating proper course ratings based on the yardage and other obstacles to the extent that they affect the scratch golfer. Don't concern yourself with the mathematics, but you should be able to pick up a scorecard and understand that a golf course with a par of 72 and a course rating of 74.1 from the back tees is going to be difficult since the scratch golfer is expected to shoot over par by 2.1 strokes. You may notice, however, that the course rating from the middle tees is only 71.8, meaning that the length of the course from the back tees is the true difficulty. Slope rating is actually the measurement of difficulty for the bogey golfer compared to the course rating. The lowest slope rating is 55 and the highest is 155. Slope ratings take into account all of the "trouble" on a golf course, since non-scratch golfers tend to find more of it. Water hazards, out-of-bounds, tree lined fairways, sloped fairways, difficult greens, forced carries, number of bunkers, fairway bunkers in landing areas, tall rough, etc. will all affect the slope rating. For example, if you come across a course with a slope rating of less than 120 you can expect a fairly simple layout. However, if you look at a card and see that the slope rating is 136 be prepared for a challenge at keeping your ball in play.

2. Architectural Tendencies

Every pro should understand how courses are designed and especially the thought processes of an architect as he develops a hole. In many cases, this process is actually done in reverse order—from the green back to the tee box. This is also an excellent way to view every hole that you play. You will be surprised how it changes your perspective. Furthermore, learn the different styles of the most popular architects because you will see them repeated all over the country, and even copied by other architects. You should know that Pete Dye (TPC at Sawgrass) loves railroad ties and blind shots, A.W. Tillinghast (Winged Foot) "buries elephants" in a lot of his greens, and Perry Maxwell (Southern Hills) and Donald Ross (Pinehurst No. 2) favor small greens that resemble upside down bowls so your landing area is actually a lot smaller than it looks like, plus, if you're not careful, you can actually putt right off one of their greens and be chipping from several yards away. Nicklaus (Muirfield Village) always played a very high left-to-right fade, so you will see a lot of his designs that require having that shot in your bag. Palmer (King's North at Myrtle Beach National) played the ball right-to-left and was a "go for broke" type of player and it shows in his course designs, as well.

Speak with the course pro, or even the superintendent *(e.g. gatekeeper)* if he is available. Ask about the subtleties and idiosyncrasies of the course, especially how it plays under the day's conditions (i.e. hot, cold, dry, wet, windy, direction of wind, etc), to gain some invaluable local knowledge. You might have several extra clubs in your trunk and want to exchange your 2-iron for a 5-wood or hybrid club if there are more forced carries to the greens than run-up shots. Anticipate problems by learning where the worst trouble (out-of-bounds, tall native grass, thick trees, unplayable lies, etc ...) is found and what is the best way to avoid it. You should already have a good working knowledge of the rules of golf, but this is also a chance to discover any local rules that might apply in a tournament situation. For instance, proper drop areas, ground under repair, unusual boundary markers, young trees with staked supports, temporary structures, new sod, and drainage systems are all good examples of local rules that may be in effect. If a member approaches you with some advice, be friendly and thank him and then throw it out the window. It is very likely that their approach to the course, and the game of golf, is very different than that of a professional. If you were a salesman for a Fortune 500 company closing deals worth millions of dollars, you wouldn't seek the advice of someone holding a garage sale, would you?

3. Geography, Climate and Grass Type

Take time to learn the geographical area and local climate where you are playing. Understand the elevation changes and how it affects your carry distance. You will need to know how temperature and humidity can affect distance, ball flight and your own swing. Our muscles will not be as flexible in the cold, plus we are bundled up with extra clothing which can shorten your swing when you don't even know it. Not to mention, colder weather also means your shafts will not flex or torque as much as normal, so you may see a loss of distance and lower ball flight. Warmer weather means the ball will go farther, but not as much when it is also really humid because the moisture in the air will slow it down. Your longest carry distances will be in the desert or at high elevations, such as in Colorado. These factors may lead you to choose a different model of ball than you normally play. In addition, know the type of grass you're playing on and the amount of rainfall the area usually receives. Hard, dry Bermuda grass in Oklahoma will mean drives that run forever, but soft, wet Rye or Fescue in New York means shorter drives that stick when they land, but then so do your approaches to the green, giving you more precision with your irons. Many courses have different grass in the greens than the fairways and rough, and it is important to find this out and understand the grain tendencies of Poa Annua (annual bluegrass) versus Zoysia, etc. Many designers use features of grass to offset landscape features. For example, grass will almost always grow towards the nearest water but a designer can fool you by making the green slope upward in the direction of the water, thereby creating grain that makes your ball seem to break uphill. However, the greatest force on the greens will usually be nearby mountains, so always know where they are and assume most putts will break away from the mountains. It is also helpful to know which direction the prevailing wind comes from and even small details such as the type of sand used in the bunkers. Your wedge does not go through coastal sand the same as the heavier types of sand found in the middle of the country.

4. Local Knowledge

While the majority of "local knowledge" to be discovered will be found within the elements described above, you can also uncover some other secrets about certain holes by talking to the pro, members or course regulars. For instance, they can give you tidbits of information like a green that is backed by thick trees and the wind will not hurt your approach shot as much as it seems from the fairway where the wind blows harder. Also, there may be holes with water to carry and the locals can tell you if the biggest hitter they know can carry a certain pond or creek from the tee. You can also find out if there's a short par-5 that actually provides more birdies to those that lay up, as opposed to those that go for the green in two. Maybe the area around the green has deep, thick rough that is difficult to chip from, so you're better off hitting in a wedge from 80–100 yards.

These are just a few examples, but you may be surprised at the wealth of knowledge that the locals possess about the course you are scheduled to play. Be smart and soak up all of the information that you can gather.

F. Warm Up Routine

As human beings we are creatures of habit. Why not create habits that help us reach our goals? No matter what your endeavor, know that the right warm up routine will make you more effective.

Sales

1. Effectively Starting Your Sales Day

Starting you sales day today means ending your sales day correctly the day before. When preparing to end your sales day, look at your calendar for tomorrow and prepare the materials and whatever else you may need for the following day. That way, when you walk into the office tomorrow, you are ready to start right away with your purpose for being in sales.

Another important way to start the day is by taking in some information about the many aspects of sales, your products/services, your company, industry or competitors. Reading two to five pages per work day means you have read 500 to 1,250 pages per year. That is a lot of information to assist in starting your day correctly.

Get in a professional sales frame of mind. This may mean not spending time socializing with those that are not determined to be the top salespeople in your organization; but that is okay. They are not paying your bills, you are.

2. Goals

Every morning review your goals for the day. Daily items included are:

Which accounts you are closing today,
How many contacts you are going to make today,
How many follow-up calls you are going to make today,
Review all of your hot prospects,
And most importantly, which accounts you are going to close today!!!!!!!

Work smart and hard at achieving your daily goals. Stay focused. You are a professional!!!

3. Sleep

A very important part of your sales day starts the night before. To be the very best you can be make sure you get an ample amount of sleep. You will be amazed at how much more productive and sharp you are when you take care of your body. So tonight, and every night, make sure you are getting the right amount of sleep for you.

Golf

1. Range

Now, you're armed with a wealth of knowledge about the course and it's time to head to the range to warm up. After a few minutes of simple stretching exercises, begin by making a few easy swings with your wedge. Hit about ten balls no more than 75–100 yards just to get loosened up. Work your way through your short irons to your long irons going incrementally (e.g. 9, 7, 5, 3 or 8, 6, 4, 2). Strictly work on your ball striking and try not to pay too much attention to ball flight. Concentrate on making clean, crisp contact every time. Depending on the amount of time you have and how much you like to practice, you may hit every club or just every other club, but the important thing is to work from short irons to long and then move on to your woods. Hit a few fairway woods and then your driver last. Make sure that the last drive you hit is a good one. Never walk away on a bad drive. You want a positive vision when you stand on the first tee.

2. Chipping Green and Practice Bunker

Next, if the course has one available, proceed to the practice chipping green where you can work on pitch shots and running chip shots to get a feel for how the ball rolls out once landing on the green's surface. Hopefully, they will have a bunker to practice in, as well.

3. Putting Green

Moving on to the practice putting green, try to find a relatively flat area of the green to begin rolling some warm up putts. First, work on one hole only. Do not putt around to every hole on the practice green. Choose a hole and remove the flag. You will not putt on the course with the pin in the cup, so you shouldn't do it in practice, either. Start by practicing a few ten foot putts just to groove your stroke in for the day and to get an idea of the stimpmeter rating of the greens. For every practice putt, be sure to hole everything out. Don't pick up the leftover one-foot or two-foot putts. You have to hole them out on the course and you should practice as closely to the on-course conditions as possible. Move around the hole in a circle, maintaining a ten foot radius, and take note of the subtle changes in the break as you change positions. Once you have come full circle, begin moving back ten feet at a time, rolling six to ten balls from twenty feet, then thirty feet and, finally, forty feet. Study the grain of the grass and concentrate on the speed. It's not important to make any of these putts. However, before you leave the practice green be sure to sink a few three-feet putts in a row to build your confidence. It's nice to hear the cup rattle. Absolutely never leave the green on a missed putt.

PRACTICAL APPLICATIONS:

Every morning when you get to the office, sitting at your desk and every time you arrive at the golf course, know that through your thorough preparation you are not only a master sales person and an improving golfer, but a well rounded individual who can and will contribute to more than just the task at hand. You may be the only one in the room or on the course who knows the secret that everyone wants to know, which is: everything you need to know about sales you can learn by playing golf. Feel confident in this knowledge and enjoy your adventure.

Chapter 2 Summary

To increase my sales I will _____!!!

To lower my score I will _____!!!

Chapter 3

Prospecting—Driving for Show and Dough

CONCEPT (Tying sales and golf together): In sales and golf, both, you begin with a wide target and slowly narrow your focus until you finally close the deal. It is essential that you are prepared for a variety of circumstances. You need to create opportunities, be comfortable in tense situations and remember to always have fun. Be consistent and the high sales commissions, as well as the low golf scores, will be consistent, too.

The first stage in the sales cycle is prospecting. In golf terms, this is your drive off of the tee. You are in control, your (sales) ball is sitting on the tee, you pick the club (your way of addressing the ball) and swing away. If you hit your drive correctly, you are sitting in the fairway and you are ready for an easier second shot. If you drive your ball into a hazard, your job just got a little harder. Let's discuss the intricacies of prospecting and driving the ball right where you want it.

A. First Tee

Now that you have fully prepared you are ready to get into the game. Whether you are looking into the eyes of your first prospect or gazing down a long, beautiful fairway the question is the same, "What am I doing here and how can I perform my very best?" Many people think that the first tee in golf or the first call of the sales day is the most difficult. For you is this fact or fiction?

Sales

1. Your First Call of the Day

As a sales professional, you have prepared for your first call of the day. You are rested and confident, knowing you will hit the sales ball into the fairway to ensure a clear look at the green. Make the call in such a way to set a strong positive tone for the day. Be aware of what is and is not in your control and respond accordingly. You will never have to react because you are prepared for whatever you encounter.

2. Cold Calling vs. Networking

There are two ways to prospect. The old school way is cold calling. In this scenario, you are going into offices or homes interrupting strangers in an attempt to raise interest for your product/service. While there is an art to cold calling, your closing percentages are improved with warm or hot calling.

Networking is nothing more than calling on not only the people you already know, but also the people they know and the people they know and so on. Whether you realize it or not you have a rather large network of people in your life, both personally and professionally. The key is to organize your network and work your network. (shameless commercial—One of the authors of this book has written two detailed books on networking—*More Leads* and *Powerful People Are Powerful Networkers*). Besides networking at Chamber of Commerce functions, utilize the networks your customers already have in place by asking two simple questions of those who have already purchased from you: 1) "Who is your favorite customer?" and 2) "Who is your favorite vendor?" By working with your customers favorites in these areas, your network will grow quickly and profitably.

There is much power in networking. Many times in my (Peter) sales career, my monthly cold calling numbers were zero but I was the leader in sales for my company. That is because networking is more effective than cold calling. Every customer can give you at least two referrals—a favorite customer and a favorite supplier (see paragraph above.) Everybody has a favorite somebody in their life. But remember, it is called net-working for a reason. Work your net and it will profit you greatly.

3. Always Be Closing

No matter where you find yourself in the sales cycle, be aware of why you are in sales—to make a sale. This means to recognize when the prospect is ready to buy and let them buy. Don't delay a sales transaction by ensuring you proceed through the sales cycle in your manner and at your pace. Every step of the way utilizes trial closes. If the prospect wants to buy before you share all of the precious information you want to share, stop sharing and start the paperwork.

4. You Are In Control

Be sure that in every stage of the sales cycle you are in control. Many times the prospect will want to take charge of the sale and buy on their terms at their price. Experienced, professional salespeople are masters at maintaining control of the sales cycle by asking questions which lead the prospect to the right conclusion, buy the product/service from them. There are great study guides and materials for you to explore as you educate yourself as a professional. Additionally, maintain control of your emotions at all times. Remember, the one who angers you controls you.

Golf

"It is not the critic who counts, not the one who points out how the strong man stumbled or how the doer of deeds might have done them better. The credit belongs to the man who is actually in the arena; whose face is marred with sweat and dust and blood; who strives valiantly; who errs and comes short again and again; who knows the great enthusiasms, the great devotions and spends himself in a worthy cause and who, if he fails, at least fails while bearing greatly so that his place shall never be with those cold and timid souls who know neither victory nor defeat."

Theodore Roosevelt
excerpt from The Man In the Arena speech

1. Preparation

Tee time! Make your way over to the first tee and get ready to start your round. Introduce yourself to the starter and greet your competitors. Exchange cards with your marker. Don't forget the small details: prepare all of your golf essentials. Make sure you have tees, a divot tool and a ball marker in your pockets. Get your glove on and then be sure to mark your ball with a distinguishing mark (usually using a felt tip pin) then show it to your competitors so they know what ball you're playing and how it is marked. Now, this may sound trite, but be sure to count your clubs and make sure that you do not have more than fourteen (remember Ian Woosnam at the British Open in 2001?). Check the wind direction, decide where you want to land the ball and with what type of trajectory. Then, choose your weapon. Study the hole and determine where the worst case scenario is and take it out of play. In other words, avoid it at all costs. If there is out-of-bounds right, then make sure the type of shot you're playing cannot go right (hook it, pull it, aim far left, whatever it takes). Get focused on the shot and block out all other thoughts. Once you are mentally prepared, go through your pre-shot routine and execute the shot. Make the vision in your head become a reality. Throughout the round, but especially on the first tee, focus on the execution not the results. If you do hit a bad shot, don't let it determine your attitude for the rest of the hole or the rest of the day. Overcome the adversity and get back on track.

2. Nerves

Many people define "luck" as preparation meeting opportunity. If you believe this definition and you want to be "lucky" in golf, then remember that practice creates muscle memory so your body can repeat the learned movements in your swing with consistency—even under pressure. When opportunity arises, you'll be ready if you're prepared for the moment. Golf is a solitary sport. Nobody else is going to hit the ball for you. Therefore, there is nobody else to blame for your mistakes, but there's also nobody that you have to share the glory with when you hit great shots. For many golfers of average ability or less, this "glory vs. embarrassment" comes at the first tee because they have difficulty hitting in front of other people. Frequently, there will be a few other golfers waiting around and watching as you tee off, plus the starter and anyone watching from the pro shop or restaurant if they have windows that face the first tee box. Everyone wants to hit a nice, smooth drive down the middle of the first fairway so as to impress the "gallery." Sometimes this pressure is too much for golfers already lacking confidence in their swing, so they choke big time and slice it into no man's land or, even worse, top a ball that dribbles up just short of the ladies' tee box. So, how do you get properly prepared to tee off? It starts with your pre-shot routine.

I (Matt) will never forget a time when my nerves got the better of me on the first tee of an important tournament. Many years ago, I was competing in a State Amateur Championship qualifier and my stomach was in knots on the first tee. I had been looking forward to this event for a long time and it meant a lot to me to play well in such a prestigious competition. I was so anxious that I failed to go through my normal mental and physical pre-shot routine, resulting in a wild hook that went out-of-bounds—a stroke and distance penalty. My heart sunk and I was completely deflated. Gathering myself, I managed to re-tee another ball and stripe it down the middle. I finished the first hole with a triple-bogey and eventually missed the cut by two shots. If I had simply put that first tee shot in play somewhere I would have, in all likelihood, made the cut and had a chance to play in the State Amateur. I have never forgotten that moment, that hole or that round and every time I begin to get nervous on the golf course I can recall that mistake and remember to slow down and go through my routine.

B. Pre-Shot Routine

How does it feel when you perform part of your job perfectly and hit the ball to within inches of where you aimed for? By repeating your sequence to these successes you eventually come up with your pre-shot routine, the events, both mental and physical, that led up to the success. Let's discuss how to find the best pre-shot routine for you.

<u>Sales</u>

1. Visualize

Before you meet with any prospect or are dealing with a customer visualize the conversation. Rehearse it in your mind. Know all of the variables that can or will arise and professionally resolve and address each professionally and thoroughly. Never put yourself in a position of being surprised. Visualize the process up to the time the prospect becomes a customer and happily gives you referrals because their order was fulfilled by you so magnificently. Don't just stop the visualization at the close of the sale. After all, you need the next sale too.

2. Assumptive

Every time you meet a prospect always assume they need your product/service, you are the best provider of what they need and there is no reason they should not buy from you. Treat them as if they already own it and the will. Never doubt. Never, never doubt!

3. Have Fun

When performed professionally, sales is the easiest and most fun career you will ever have. You will also work harder than you ever have, but with a smile on your heart. If you project you are having fun, your prospect will have fun. Maybe they are never around others having fun at what they do for a living. Having fun could be like a breath of fresh air for your prospect. Having fun also makes your day go by much faster and easier. It may even increase your sales.

Golf

1. Get in Your Comfort Zone

You may be thinking, "What makes a good pre-shot routine?" Well, that's a difficult question to answer because everybody's routine will be a little different because it should contain personal elements that get you into your comfort zone. Some routines even contain superstitions and odd behavior, but it's not important that your routine be reasonable to the onlooker—it only has to be effective. Pre-shot routines may even start with what you have in your pockets and whether they're in the left or right pocket. Many golfers prefer to always take their tee from the right pocket, so it's important for them to make sure that pocket remains stocked with the proper number of tees.

2. Visualize

Once you have the ball teed up at the proper height and on the appropriate side of the teeing area for the shot you want to play, the first element of any good routine should be to visualize your shot. You have probably heard this concept mentioned quite often from instructors, players and authors but most golfers never really grasp it. You really have to quiet your mind by blocking out all distractions and focus tightly on the hole, or shot in front of you. Envision yourself making the perfect swing and then the ball taking flight from your club on the precise trajectory that you intended, including a draw or fade, rising to the crest of its trajectory angle and then falling towards your target and landing softly, landing hard and running forward, or landing and spinning back—whatever the desired result may be that will get the ball to stop where you want it.

In other words, you have to picture the entire shot, start to finish, and then step up to the ball and make your vision become reality. This is a very important moment when it is essential to be realistic with yourself and know your limitations. If you consistently play a low trajectory and have a hard time hitting the high, soft shots then all the "mental focus" in the world is not going to make you hit a high, soft ball. That part comes from your physical practice and swing changes. The mental focus you need to visualize a particular shot is actually much harder to obtain and utilize effectively. As a matter of fact, if you have two golfers of equal physical ability and talent then you will usually find that what truly separates them is mental strength and focus—usually referred to as *mental toughness*. You can learn mental toughness, though, with time and practice. Start at the range by trying to visualize each shot before you make every swing. Keep picturing the same shot until you can actually hit it at least five times in a row. Then, move on to visualizing a different type of shot. In the beginning, you may spend your entire range session trying to hit one shot five times in a row and that's okay—just don't give up. You will never achieve anything worthwhile without unwavering perseverance.

3. Every Detail Must Be Consistent

Once you have mastered the art of visualization, the next few parts of your pre-shot routine may consist of seemingly frivolous things such as hitching up your pants, pulling up your shirt sleeve, adjusting your hat or sunglasses, or twisting the club in your hands. These are all little things that may appear silly and pointless, but they are very important to the individual; therefore, they need to be repeated before every shot in exactly the same manner. Some golfers will stand a few feet behind the ball to make their practice swings, while others may like to practice while addressing the ball. Some people will pay close attention to the mechanics of their practice swings and others will swing just to loosen up and get a feel for the shot. Many golfers actually choose not to make a practice swing, at all. Some will waggle the club a few times and others will pull the trigger quickly. Just remember that, no matter what you do to feel comfortable and get focused, you need to be consistent and do the exact same thing every time.

C. Driving the Ball

Driving the ball, a.k.a. prospecting, demands a commitment to excellence. You only get one chance to make that first impression. Will you land in the fairway, ready to make that sale, or visit a hazard, making the next shot that much more of a challenge (a.k.a.—a learning experience)?

Sales

1. Sales is Easier than Golf

Professional sales is easier than golf for this reason: when you are standing on the first tee is everyone, including those not in your foursome, staring at you? Has a group ever stared at you in public when you sell? Probably not. You can easily perform sales in any weather condition. Golf is usually weather variable. In golf you need specific equipment to start. In sales you need only you to start. Golf is a four letter word, sales is not. People get frustrated in golf and throw their clubs. Have you ever heard of a salesperson getting frustrated and throwing a salesperson? The next time you get frustrated with sales, remember, sales is easier than golf.

2. Different "Drives" as You Walk Through the Door

When you walk through the door you have the constants of your company, your product/service and you. On the other side of the door you have the variables of the people you are dealing with and the unpredictable things they are facing. All of these variables can be easily taken into account by knowing many ways to approach the same person depending on their situation at the time. Just as you would address and hit a golf ball to take into account the placement of a tree with respect to the green, you should have in your sales repertoire a variety of ways to address your prospects. Remember, making a positive first impression is the same as driving a golf ball a long way down the middle of the fairway.

Golf

Since this chapter focuses on driving the ball, we will devote some time to offer a few tips that will help you build confidence with your driver. Having completed your custom fitting session, it's time to go to the range and practice with your new driver, but get away from those mats with the rubber tees. Find a spot at the end of the range where they have natural grass and use your wood tees just like you will on the golf course.

1. Controlled Drive

It's good to have two types of drives in your swing repertoire. First, work on the controlled drive that may give up a few yards but will usually find the fairway. You must have this shot for tight driving holes and especially windy conditions when big, flowing swings can get you blown off balance, easily. Second, work on your "swing for the fences" drive that you can use on wide open shots, during purely recreational rounds where your score is not really important to you, or even for fun in scrambles when you don't have to play it if it ends up in a bad spot.

Let's first point out that you will not ever achieve the long bomb without first learning how to hit the sweet spot of the club head the majority of the time. Therefore, the controlled, consistent shot with your driver needs to be addressed first. Besides, we all know that this game is much easier when played from the fairway, so let's learn how to keep the ball in the short stuff.

The controlled drive should start with a relatively narrow stance. As you address the ball, your toes should be pointed slightly outward and your heels should not be farther apart than the width of your shoulders. Focus on rhythm, tempo, and swinging through the ball.

2. Power Drive

The "big" drive starts with a wider stance. This provides a better foundation for a hard swing and, ultimately, better balance. Focus on a smooth takeaway—don't jerk the club back quickly—and the acceleration through the impact zone. Generally speaking, you will want to place the ball slightly farther ahead in your stance to promote catching the ball on your upswing, thus increasing carry distance.

3. Working the Ball

When you have these two swings grooved in your muscle memory and you're confident over either one, you may want to practice "working" the ball. Golf becomes a lot easier when you have the confidence to play a fade one hole, then a draw on the next, working your way around the course exactly the way the architect intended. However, for our purposes, let's concentrate on the first two types of drives mentioned.

4. Know Your Limits

On the course, the most important part of being a good driver is to know your limits. Often, you will ask a golfer what he averages off the tee and the number that he provides is usually a lot closer to where his good drives land, not his average ones. *(Note: that the golfer is being referred to as "he" because this tendency is mainly confined to men. Women are much more honest about their games. Men tend to judge each other's masculinity by how far they can hit a golf ball. Ironically, in sales there is no distinction between men and women—they both fudge their statistics equally. Ask a salesperson how their recent sales are going and they'll be sure to tell you about the big one they closed, but they might leave out the fact that their monthly average is not that great.)* It is important to know what your true average is, not just how far it goes when you hit it perfect and the conditions provide no resistance (i.e. uphill, into the wind, rain, cold, etc.). For instance, if you average 250 yards with your driver, don't try to carry a creek that requires 235 yards of carry distance to clear it. Statistically, you won't make it most of the time because your normal drive probably carries 220–230 yards in the air and rolls out to 250 yards total. Know your limits and play smart. Golf is a game of patience and, at the end of the day, you will be rewarded.

5. Alignment

The same honesty plays a big part in your address. As you step up to the ball and begin to choose your aiming point, be honest with yourself and know your game. Don't aim down the middle if you know that you usually have a 10–15 yard fade. Aim left, confidently, and play for the ball to fade back to the center of the fairway. Bruce Lietzke has made a career out of being honest with himself and his swing. Throughout his years on the PGA Tour, and now on the Champions Tour, he consistently aims down the left side of the fairway, or even at the left rough, and confidently cuts the ball back into the middle of the short grass. There's nothing wrong with a big cut shot so long as you believe in it and allow for it at setup.

When you're driving the golf ball, don't just aim at the entire fairway. Pick a small target or specific side of the fairway and make that your target. If you aim wide you'll miss even wider. If you aim narrow your misses will be more controlled and will usually avoid any possible trouble areas that are wide left or right. Focusing on a small target should be an integral part of your pre-shot routine that we discussed in Chapter 2.

PRACTICAL APPLICATIONS:

Every day know that your sales territory is like a well manicured fairway. Just pick the place to drive your "sales ball" too and enjoy the trip to the "green", where the ball is putted into the hole and the sale is consummated.

When golfing, as you stand on the tee ready to drive the ball, look at the fairway and see your sales prospects, some great, a few "rough" and maybe even "hazardous". Know which prospects are profitable and drive the ball there. You will then be ready for a great second shot.

Chapter 3 Summary

To increase my sales I will _____!!!

To lower my score I will _____!!!

Chapter 4

Qualifying—Eyeing the Green

CONCEPT (Tying sales and golf together): After initial prospecting you begin narrowing your focus to the prospects that are truly potential clients. It is the same in golf as your target narrows from a wide fairway to the green. Whether it's sales or golf, this is where you decide if you will benefit more from an aggressive or conservative approach. It is now that you create your sales/scoring opportunity.

It is important to be in control of yourself physically, mentally and emotionally. Learn to use your past experiences to your benefit. There are times when good memories will help you and other times when a bad experience can turn into a positive as it guides you to a better decision this time.

The next step in the sales cycle is to qualify the situation in front of you to see if you are staring at a prospect or a suspect. Whether you are in golf or in sales, you are eyeing the "green," be it the money or the putting surface. How do you get the ball to where it is supposed to go?

A. Narrowing Your Focus

No matter what you do, you are doing it with your goal in mind: close the sale, get the ball onto the green. Distractions are not allowed. Do your job with that single focus.

Sales

1. What are Your Qualifying Questions?

You have prospected and are now talking with someone who wants to talk with you. Your job is to discover whether they are a prospect who has a need you can fulfill or a suspect who is going to waste your most non-renewable resource—your time.

Every industry has a series of questions that are asked in order to find the level of interest as well as the appropriate product/service for the prospect. The questions will also eliminate those people that are time wasters, suspects rather than true prospects. In addition, the questions may show some other concerns or needs never previously thought about by either you or the prospect.

Learn not only your qualifying questions, but how to ask the same question in at least three ways. This will ensure you are thorough and the questions will be understood by people of different backgrounds and perspectives. It also helps to clarify positions.

Take a moment right now and list your most effective qualifying question on a sheet of paper or in the back cover if this book. You can add to the list by asking those most successful in your company and industry to share with you the qualifying questions they have found to be most effective. Share your questions with them to fine tune your list.

2. Building a Relationship

Learn how to ask your qualifying question in a very relaxed and conversational manner. You are not an interrogator, but are developing a relationship, that if done properly, will flow into the next stage of the sales cycle and result in a sale for you and joy for your prospect as they graduate to the title of customer. In addition, the person sitting in front of you has a network of individuals and companies that may be in need of your product/service either now or in the future. Build a long-lasting relationship. It will offer both of you dividends for years.

Golf

Eliminate negative thoughts and find a positive approach to all challenges. Consider the hazards on a golf course to simply be challenges that can be overcome or avoided. You can hit over hazards to close the deal quicker, but sometimes it's smarter to simply play safe and eventually close the deal in the long run.

When you are preparing to hit your approach shot, don't just aim for the green and hope; learn to aim for the pin or use an object in the distance that provides a small target. Many times, you may not even want to go directly at the pin, so be sure that you know where the best part of the green is from which to putt to the pin position and dial in the shot with precision.

1. Broad vs. Small Target

The important part is to narrow your focus. In golf, even when you have a wide target area, do not aim for a broad target. Always aim for the smallest possible target you can focus in on. If you're on the tee box and you have a huge, wide fairway in front of you then find a portion of the fairway to focus on and convince yourself that it is the only place you can land your ball. It could be a discolored area of grass, a hump in the fairway, a spot beyond a bunker that you intend to carry or maybe a telephone pole in the distance on the same line that you want to hit the ball. Whatever it is, fixate on it and then swing away and let your body complete the visual picture that your brain has painted for you.

The reason you want a small target is two-fold. First, it helps intensify your focus and block out all other distractions. Second, if you miss your aiming point then you are more likely to still be in good shape. In other words, if your target is fifty yards wide and you miss then you are likely to be ten to thirty yards out of the fairway. However, if your aiming point is only three yards wide then you can miss your target by twenty yards and still be in the fairway. This is not a new concept. Pros have been teaching this philosophy for decades, but most amateurs have a hard time maintaining the mental discipline it takes to implement it for an entire round. If you stay focused and work hard at it, you can make this concept part of your natural routine on every shot and it will improve your game, no question about it.

2. Aggressive vs. Conservative (Decision Making)

When you have taught yourself to narrow your focus on every shot, then you can begin to utilize it in your game plan. This art of visualization is useful in the aggressive parts of your round as well as the conservative portions. When you decide to play an aggressive shot over a hazard, for example, find a small target and be committed to the shot that you have envisioned and the club you have selected. If you stay focused then even a mis-hit should stay in play and hopefully you can recover. Ironically, the time when most golfers don't pay enough attention is on the easy shots. When you decide to play conservatively and hit a 3-wood off the tee or lay up a second shot in the fairway, don't get too relaxed just because it's not a pressure shot. The easy shots count as one stroke just like the difficult ones, so go through the same process every time.

3. Scoring Opportunity

If you want to learn how to shoot low scores, then the most important time to narrow your focus is when scoring opportunities arise. In other words, anytime you have the chance to get the ball close to the hole, or in the hole, your target may be as small as a spot on the green no bigger than a quarter. When chipping, pitching or playing from a bunker, pick a small spot on the green where you want the ball to land or roll over and block out everything else around you and focus on getting the ball to that point. This is especially effective when playing a course with severely undulated greens because many times you may find yourself chipping or putting to a specific spot that is 10 or 20 feet from the hole, allowing for the ball to run out of speed and break in toward the hole.

Think about the last time that you had your eye on the green, focused in on the pin, took dead aim, remained calm and pulled off the exact shot that you envisioned in your mind. Let's say that the shot was a beautiful, high draw with a 7-iron that started at the right edge of the green and slowly curled back toward the left pin position, landed six feet right of the pin, and spun left to leave a simple, uphill three foot putt for birdie. As majestic as that sounds, you probably envisioned that shot several other times that day and didn't come close to executing it. Well, if you did it almost every time, golf would become boring, right? Wrong. You'd probably be cashing paychecks on the PGA Tour, assuming that your 7-iron isn't the only club in your bag that you can hit with any consistency.

B. Consistency

The beauty about both sales and golf is that when you are consistent in the way you go through every step of the process, you will be consistent in reaping the rewards and reaching your goals. Do it right, do it often, and do it the same proven successful way every time. This is easy, right?

Sales

1. Emotional

In sales, consistency is very important. Your prospects and customers should feel secure because they are dealing with the same person on a regular basis, not just someone that looks the same and has the same name as the person they built a relationship with. As a salesperson it is important to maintain a positive professional demeanor no matter what turmoil is going on around you or inside of you. Only your prospects and customers have the liberty of going all over the emotional landscape. You are to be a constant in their lives; you should be a constant for the better. This is one reason why it is so important to have a positive and consistent routine to begin your sales day. By being emotionally consistent for yourself, you are being emotionally consistent for those around you. Remember, people buy emotionally and justify logically. Help them to buy by being consistent emotionally.

2. Logical

Be consistent in what you say and how you say it. If you do not have an answer to a question, acknowledge that it was a great question and that you will get back to them with the correct answer. Again, the consistency of starting your sales day with a productive routine will aid you, your prospects and your customers in a tremendous way. Because people justify their purchases logically, your consistency in this area will help eliminate buyer's remorse and increase your referral base.

Golf

1. Muscle Memory

It's a well known fact that consistency is truly the key to better golf. A good swing comes from your body's ability to create muscle memory, which is your ability to consistently repeat the same movement—time after time, especially under pressure. That's why you hear the announcers on TV constantly noting the importance of a player staying in their routine. The most important muscle memory we create is between our ears. Our minds work in conjunction with our bodies to make our actions more easily repeatable the more often we do them. Your brain remembers and so do your muscles. The same is true for throwing a football or a baseball, serving a tennis ball, or shooting a free throw. This concept is not new. So, if every professional golfer understands this, why don't more amateurs get it? It's not really a secret and nobody has a patent on it, but most amateurs either don't pay attention to it or they don't even know about this simple concept.

The ideal golf swing is one that repeats every time and delivers the club head back at impact exactly the way it was at setup. There are many different types of swings but the one thing that all of the good ones have in common is the repeatability and consistency of the process. Muscle memory is the source of every good golf swing on the planet. So, find a swing that works for you and then teach your body to repeat it every time and you will have found the key to hitting more fairways and greens.

2. Selective Memory

When it comes to both muscle memory and your brain's memory, it is helpful to practice the art of selective memory. Essentially, just forget your bad shots and remember your good ones. It sounds so simple but it's so hard to accomplish. When you step up to a tee box where you hit a ball in the water or out-of-bounds the last time you played the course, it is extremely difficult to block that mental picture out of your mind, but you must do it if you intend to hit a good shot this time. If you have a hard time envisioning the last time you hit a good shot on the hole, or if it's your first time playing the course, then select your club and try to remember the best shot you ever hit with that particular club and then step up and make it happen, again.

For instance, every time I (Matt) pull out my 7-iron I remember a fantastic high draw that I hit a few years ago as my approach shot on a par-4 at my home course. I visualize that majestic shot that ended up only three feet from the pin, little more than a tap-in birdie, on the hardest hole on the course. I was playing with my regular weekend gambling group and I'm sure that they, too, have never forgotten that shot as it cost them a considerable amount of money to witness. Each and every time I swing my 7-iron I am trying to recreate that shot and, surprisingly, I am able to do it on occasion.

As golfers, it is in our nature to be hard on ourselves and, frequently, be pessimistic about our game. The path to better golf, though, is only paved with positive stepping stones. There is no room for negativity. You must train yourself to be optimistic about every round, every hole and every shot. When you hit a bad shot just forget about it and move forward as best you can. When you hit good shots you need to log them in your memory bank for future withdrawal in pressure situations. Then, and only then, will you be able to improve and move forward with your golf game.

PRACTICAL APPLICATIONS:

In sales, know that asking the right qualifying question is the same as choosing the correct club out of your golf bag. Know the tendencies of each club (qualifying question), and how to hit (ask) each club correctly, and you will learn quickly if the person in front of you is a true prospect, or just a suspect wasting your time (get referrals either way!!!).

On the golf course ask yourself the right questions to choose the right club. Remember that in both golf and sales the goal is still the same: obtain the best information to make the right choice to attain the goal at hand.

Chapter 4 Summary

To increase my sales I will _____!!!

To lower my score I will _____!!!

Chapter 5

Presentations—Your Second Shot

CONCEPT (Tying sales and golf together): As a salesperson, when you make your presentation you are being evaluated by the client, but you should also be assessing them. It is the same in golf when it comes to hitting your approach shot to the green. You must be assessing the situation while, at the same time, the golf course is providing an evaluation of you in the form of your ability to produce scoring opportunities. Will you give yourself a good chance at birdie or an easy par? Or, will you have to scramble from a difficult position? Sales professionals, and golfers, face this process multiple times every day.

To be successful in either sales or golf, you will need to have a vision of your strategy, maintain control of the situation, always be planning ahead and then learn when to go for it and when to play safe.

You've made a magnificent drive (great prospecting), you are looking at the green (excellent qualifying,) and now it is time to hit the ball, that memorable and professional presentation.

A. Approach Shot

Depending on the circumstances, the type of second shot/presentation may vary. The best approach to the shot may be from the left, right, high or low, maybe a draw, spin or fade. This is same with your presentation. It must be tailored for the situation. You don't want your ball/presentation to land in a hazard guarding the green.

Sales

1. Presentation Goals

While the obvious goal of your presentation is to position your sales ball to close the sale, the unwritten goal is to close the door to the competition. The format and force of the presentation will vary depending how quickly you can close the sale. Let's look at three types of sales as they relate to golf.

2. Par-4 Sales—Two Call Close

On a golf course, par 4 holes usually make up 56% of the total holes you will play. With that in mind, make it your goal to close sales in two calls, the initial call and then the second call which includes your full presentation and a close. Sink that sales putt in regulation. To not do so puts you in a sales bogey situation. The more proficient and professional you are in every stage of the sales cycle, the more par sales you will make.

3. Par-5 Sales—3+ Calls to Close

Par 5 holes make up 22% of the holes on a golf course. Be sure that your percentage of sales that are not closed after three calls stays in the same percentages. Again, your sales cycle proficiency will help improve your closing ratio.

4. Par-3 Sales—One Call Close

There are some products and services that can be closed in one call. Like par 5 holes, par 3's also account for 22% of the holes on a golf course. Continue your mastery of sales and play all holes like a par 3. Close early, close often. Sales par on this hole is a hole-in-one.

Golf

First, know where not to hit your ball. In other words, what is the hardest place to recover from, or what is the greatest penalty, if you happen to mis-hit your shot. If you can successfully avoid the worst case scenario it will take the "big" number out of play. Ben Hogan used to say that playing great golf is not about how good your good shots are but, instead, how bad are your bad shots?

Assuming that you have successfully negotiated your tee shot and have found the fairway, you now have distinct options available for your second shot. Let's talk about your options on a par 4 hole first and then we'll discuss the strategy on a par 5. Regardless of the hole, however, always remember the process of viewing the hole from the green to the tee. Where's the best position to putt from? Usually, from below the hole with as little break as possible. Now, imagine walking backward from that spot to your position in the fairway and visualize the shot, or shots, needed to reach the desired position on the green (refer to *visualization* in Chapter 3). Certain pin placements require high, left-to-right fades to get the ball close, and others may call for a low, right-to-left run-up shot.

1. Par-4 Strategy

On a par 4, reaching the green in regulation means your ball has come to rest on the putting surface with your second shot. Depending upon the length of the hole, weather conditions, course design features and your length off the tee, you could be hitting any club in your bag from a lob wedge to a 3-wood for your second shot. Obviously, your strategy is different at both ends of that club selection spectrum. If you have any wedge in your hand you should be taking dead aim at the pin almost every time. On the other hand, if you're far enough back that you've got a fairway wood in your hands then your thought process needs to include a bailout area and the elimination of major trouble.

a. Visualize the Hole In Reverse: Green To Tee Box

In life, you can learn to see things in a new perspective by "walking a mile in someone else's shoes." On the golf course, you can gain a fantastic new perspective by walking backwards 200 to 550 yards in your own shoes. Many architects actually design their courses by starting with the green and working backwards. Obviously, you can really only achieve this if you have played the course before and you know what the entire hole looks like. Assuming you have, however, played the course before, use this reverse perspective to your advantage.

Have you ever hit a shot and thought that it was perfect only to reach your ball and find out that it is really not in that great of shape? Standing at your ball you can look back and say "Oh yeah, I should've hit it over there, instead." When hitting tee shots and approach shots, try to visualize the hole as if you are standing on the green and looking back toward where your ball lies. This can be an invaluable tool in your mental repertoire.

b. Green Light Situations

Anytime you find yourself in the fairway with less than 150 yards to the pin, you should consider this a "green light" situation, assuming you're not blocked out by a tree or other obstruction. The "green light" means you are cleared to "go" for the pin and try to knock one close for a legitimate birdie opportunity. For the average golfer, this will mean you are hitting 7-iron or less. So how do you gain the confidence with your short irons that will allow you to see these situations as "green light" opportunities? The answer is distance control. Distance control is what separates the great ball-strikers from the good ones.

c. Distance Control

The first step to gaining distance control is to learn your **true** distances with each of your irons. This means practicing enough to know how far the ball will carry, release and/or spin back with each club.

i. Short Irons

Most golfers are not honest when it comes to judging distance. If I ask the average amateur how far he hits his 8-iron and he responds "150 yards," then it probably means that his absolute best 8-iron flies 147 yards and releases about three yards. It's funny, though, that if you see him play a shot that requires a 145 yard carry over water to a pin that is cut on the front of the green, he's probably hitting a 7-iron—not the 8-iron—because he doesn't trust that he'll pull off that flush 8-iron shot that he claims he hits 150 yards. Don't get me wrong—he's made the right decision by hitting 7-iron, but the important factor to note is that he needs to know his true distance with his 8-iron and not just how far his best 8-iron travels. His *true* average distance is most likely around 142 carry yards with three to five yards of release. If you want to learn how to take dead aim at pins with your short irons then you must know these subtle differences in your game. In addition, you must know how to adjust your distances for wind, weather, climate and turf conditions, as well as elevation changes.

ii. Mid To Long Irons

As you move into your middle and long irons, your distance control will not be as precise but it is every bit as important. Specifically, you really need to know the carry distance of your long irons because your total distance will include a lot more release after landing than your short irons. Knowing your average carry distance with the long irons will save you plenty of strokes on long approaches over hazards. It's also important to note that your flushed shots with your 3-iron are going to add more yards than a flushed shot with your wedge. The reason is the loft of the club. When you flush your wedge, you will mostly be creating more backspin and the ball's height will be increased more than the length. A typical 3-iron has less than half the loft of a pitching wedge; therefore, when you hit a 3-iron on the sweet spot you will see more distance.

d. 150–200 Yard Approach Shots

If you are left with a second shot that is between 150–200 yards, typically a club between your 7-iron and 3-iron, then your strategy needs to change. Usually, this is not a distance from which you will be expecting to knock a shot within ten feet of the pin. Therefore, take your pin location into account and try to figure out which side of the hole will be the easiest to putt from, while also eliminating the difficult up-and-down par save if you miss the green. In fact, most golfers would see a significant improvement in their scores if they aimed solely at the middle of the green every time they found themselves within the 150–200 yard range. It may not be much fun aiming at the middle of the green but it is a smart, sure strategy for making pars and avoiding trouble.

e. 200+ Yard Approach Shots

For those long par 4's where you find yourself hitting second shots from over 200 yards out, usually with a fairway wood or hybrid club, your strategy must be more defensive. Your chances of hitting the green are significantly reduced so you need to pay close attention to the worst case scenarios. Your goal should be the middle of the green, but be sure that a mis-hit avoids any water, trees, out-of-bounds, bunkers or even just a short sided up-and-down attempt. From 200-plus yards, you will miss the green more often than you will find it so plan for the easiest par save available. Even if you hit the green with a fairway wood it may not hold the green because of a lower trajectory and reduced spin, so make sure you know what lies beyond the green.

f. Par-4 Summary

In summary, on par 4's your second shot strategy depends on the distance between the ball and the hole and the degree of distance control that you have from the fairway. From less than 150 yards, it's a "green light" situation and you should go for the pin. From 150–200 yards, aim for the best side of the pin to putt from or just the middle of the green and expect to be putting for birdie from 30-plus feet. From over 200 yards out, simply aim for the middle of the green and be sure to take the most serious trouble out of play. You may not be putting for birdie but you should expect to make par most of the time.

2. Par-5 Strategy

Now, let's discuss strategic options on par 5's.

a. Plan While On The Tee Box For Second Shot

As with any golf hole, start planning your approach to the green before you select a club on the tee. However, the par 5s include an extra element: whether or not you plan to play for the green in two or three shots. If you know that even your best drive will not put you in position to reach the green in two, then consider a different club off the tee than your driver. Granted, if the tee shot is fairly wide open and free of hazards, go ahead and hit the driver so that you can lay up with a shorter club on your second shot. However, if it's a tight shot with out-of-bounds, water, or trees in play then use a fairway wood or long iron off the tee to get the ball safely in play. Many players wonder why it is generally easier to hit a 3-wood than a driver. There are two reasons why: clubface loft and shaft length. First, the average driver has about 10.5 degrees of loft in the face while the average 3-wood will have 15 degrees. With less loft in the driver you have a flatter clubface; therefore, it imparts less backspin and more sidespin than your 3-wood. So, if you happen to mis-hit a ball, given the exact same swing and exact same contact on the face with both clubs, the shot with the driver is more likely to impart sidespin and end up farther off the intended line than the ball hit with the 3-wood. Second, the shaft on your driver can be anywhere from 1.5–4 inches longer than your 3-wood. Longer shafts provide greater distance but they are harder to control and require more precise timing, so the 3-wood becomes your "control" club off the tee.

b. Be Able To Adjust Your Plan

If a well struck driver will put you within striking distance of the green, and the risk is reasonable and within your capabilities, then hit the big stick and be confident that you can create a scoring opportunity. You must, nonetheless, have a game plan that allows for adjustments after evaluating the position in which you find your drive. If you hit the drive you wanted and can reach the green with your second shot, then stick to the original game plan and go for it. In contrast, your strategy must be adjusted to include an effective lay up and short iron approach if you don't get the distance you expected off the tee.

c. Going For The Green

So, let's say that you did hit a good drive and are well within range to go for the green with your second shot. Now your strategy is the same as previously discussed when hitting to par-4 greens from over 200 yards away. Aim for the middle of the green and be sure to take the most serious trouble out of play if you mis-hit the shot. Your goal should be to have any kind of putt for eagle, or a relatively simple up-and-down for birdie. No matter what, do not turn a scoring opportunity into a bogey or worse due to poor planning or course management. Poor execution is going to happen from time to time and you just have to try and recover, but your mental approach can be flawless every time if you work at it.

There are times, however, when the risk may seem great but you decide to go for it, anyway, because the safe play is also difficult to execute. For example, recently I was playing my home course and I came to the par-5 ninth hole at four under par so I was feeling very confident. It is a relatively short, dogleg right with an ominous bunker guarding the corner and tall trees to the right. Feeling good about my game, I tried to hit my tee shot over the bunker and trees and cut the corner but ended up fading the shot too much and was faced with a second shot with nothing but trees between me and the green. If I chose to play safe, I would have been forced to chip the ball out sideways and would have been left with over 200 yards for my third shot. Since there was no water or out-of-bounds that came into play, and my ball was on a slight uphill lie helping me to get it up and over the trees quickly, I decided to go for the green. The shot called for a high, hooking ball that would need to carry several trees and then a high-faced bunker in front of the green and approximately 215 yards to the middle of the green and the pin was in the back. I pulled out my trusty 4-wood and executed the shot to perfection, leaving myself a 40-foot putt for eagle which I subsequently drained for a front-nine 30. Playing aggressively paid off this time and I had my personal best nine-hole score. The important thing to note, though, are the three main reasons that I went for the green: 1) the lay up shot was not easy and could potentially make par very difficult to achieve, 2) if I missed the shot I was attempting it would've gone wide right and there was relatively little trouble over there, and 3) I had played very well to that point so my confidence was high and my swing was sound.

d. Laying Up

If you chose to play this par-5 conservatively, or just did not sufficiently connect with your tee shot, then an intelligent lay-up is the next shot to be played. What defines an "intelligent" lay-up? It consists of a carefully calculated club selection that will leave you with an approach shot from your "perfect" distance (the length of shot over which you feel most confident). Usually, this yardage is somewhere between 80–125 yards, but it is completely subjective. The only thing that determines the perfect distance is your own personal shot preference. Therefore, do not automatically pull out your 3-wood and try to knock the ball as close to the green as possible, leaving yourself an unmanageable half-swing with your wedge. If you feel comfortable and confident with a pitching wedge from 110 yards, then calculate your lay-up and hit your second shot to the 110-yard area. We all watch the touring pros do this on TV every weekend but it has never caught on with amateurs. It is a very effective way to maximize your scoring opportunities and a valuable lesson on course management that you get for free by watching the world's best players on TV.

One very important thing to remember when laying up: *LAY THE BALL UP SAFELY.* The lay-up shot is, by definition, the safe shot. However, amateurs are constantly trying to lay up five or ten yards short of a hazard. Why even bring the trouble into play? Figure the distance to reach the trouble, determine which club you can hit that far and then hit two or three clubs less to safely lay up behind the hazard. It's a risk/reward loss when you go for the green and end up in trouble, but it's just a complete mental breakdown to lose strokes when all you're trying to do is lay up.

e. Third Shot

Now that you have done all of the math, chosen the right club and hit the perfect lay up to your comfort zone, it's time to focus on scoring and hit your approach in tight. Let's say, for example, that you left yourself 80 yards because that's a perfect sand wedge for you. The same rule for approach shots still applies: visualize the shot starting from the spot on the green where you want to finish and working your way back to the point where your ball lies now. See the trajectory, the ball fading left to right, carrying the front bunker, spinning to a stop and tucking itself about eight feet under the pin for an easy birdie putt. Then, step up and hit the shot you've just visualized. In theory, it sounds simple. That's because it is simple to plan and will become simpler to execute through practice and development of the proper mental approach to the game. Soon, you will be carving out pars and birdies as you dissect golf courses. Precision and solid course management, among other things, are fundamental keys to long-term success as a professional golfer.

3. Par-3 Strategy

While your strategy on a par-3 is obviously simpler, you still need a plan or disaster can find you in a hurry. Essentially, a typical par-3 strategy will be just like the approach plans to the par-4 and par-5 noted above. If it's less than 150 yards, consider it a scoring opportunity and go for the pin in most cases. For holes that are 150+, develop a plan for making par with an outside chance of making a long putt for birdie. This plan needs to include recognizing where the worst trouble lies and avoiding it. It is extremely important to avoid hazards on a par-3 because it is more difficult to save even a bogey, much less a par. If you hit into the water off the tee on a par-4 then you can still drop a ball, knock it on the green and have a putt for par or a simple 2-putt for bogey. On a par-3, if you hit your tee shot in the water then you will have to drop (or even re-tee in many cases) and try to get up and down in two shots just to save bogey. So, play smart and only be aggressive when you have a short club in your hand and you feel confident with your ball striking that day. Otherwise, you can end up costing yourself a big number on a short hole.

PRACTICAL APPLICATIONS:

Whether you are selling or golfing you can always tell how well your presentation went, either by the roar of the crowd, or the kind and enthusiastic words from your prospects and peers. When making a world class sales presentation, imagine you are hitting the ball from the fairway to the green, stopping just inches from the hole, or maybe even in the hole.

On the golf course, know that your approach shot will bring cheers from your "gallery", even if just in your head.

Chapter 5 Summary

To increase my sales I will _____!!!

To lower my score I will _____!!!

Chapter 6

Handling Objections—Avoiding Hazards

CONCEPT (Tying sales and golf together): It is good advice, in general, to avoid hazards whenever possible, but it is especially important with regard to your sales game and your golf game. You must be able to identify potential hazards/objections, prepare for them, and have an effective response ready to help you handle them.

If you are properly prepared you will be able to remain calm in the face of adversity, be patient and then stay focused enough to get past any objection that the client may throw at you or any hazard that the golf course puts between you and the hole.

In a perfect world, the words of sales eloquence would roll effortlessly off our tongue and through our lips. All golf shots would land and roll only on the fairways and greens.

WAKE UP!!!!! Enjoy the dream you just had? Reality tells us that in everything we do we will run into some difficulty. The most important thing to do is ensure that all situations are handled professionally and promptly. Do not make a bad situation worse by following up a bad shot or word with a dumb one. Just get the ball, both golf and sales, back in play and avoid more hazards. Don't make a bad shot worse by making two bad shots in a row. Don't talk too much or say the wrong thing. To quote Harry S. Truman—"Never kick a fresh turd on a hot day." Smell the picture?

Sales

1. Preparation

To perfect your stroke, how many times do you practice hitting the ball out of the rough or the sand? Many!!! And then a few more!!! It is the same when professionally, and effectively, handling objections. There are great sales resources that show you how to properly address any objection you will ever encounter. Not only read these resources, but practice handling objections by role playing with co-workers, friends, customers, and your car's rear view mirror. You can never prepare enough in this area because, just when you think you have prepared enough, a prospect will present you with an objection in a manner never before experienced.

2. Anticipation

While we never want to think we will hit the ball into a hazard, knowing that we will assists us in dealing with the situation in a manner that will help, not hinder, our progress in getting the ball into the cup. In sales, know that you are going to experience sales objections. The proper mindset is to acknowledge that the prospect is asking the question because they simply want more information from which to acquire your product or service. Happily and professionally provide them with the information and close the sale. After all, that is why you are there.

3. Listening vs. Hearing

When you are faced with an objection, understand there is a difference between listening and hearing. Listening is a physical and logical act. Many times while listening we are doing nothing more than formulating what we will say when the prospect has to inhale while talking.

Hearing consists of truly understanding what the prospect is communicating, both logically and emotionally. The best way to ensure you are hearing is to restate the objection to the prospect for verification that you understand what is being conveyed. Only after agreement is obtained that you understand the objection can you actually answer the objection. Not before. If you want to obtain an evaluation of how well a hearer you are, discuss this section with family, friends, co-workers, and customers. Ask them to grade you on your proficiency in listening versus hearing. Adjust as needed.

4. Build Objections into Your Sales Presentation

Based on the experiences of yourself or others in your industry, there are some objections you know you will encounter on a regular basis. Instead of waiting for the prospect to bring up the objection (just as the last prospect did) include the objection complete with answer in your presentation. Not only will you appear to be better prepared, thorough, and professional, you will be one step closer to the sale.

Golf

1. Nerves

It's been said that the anticipation of death is much worse than death itself. With a few exceptions, this is usually true. The same theory can be applied to golf. Sometimes the anticipation of a difficult or high pressure shot can be the hardest thing to overcome. Nerves are a sure form of trouble to any golfer. One of the best ways to handle nerves is by executing your pre-shot routine and blocking out distractions. Another effective way to conquer your nervous anticipation is by concentrating your efforts on "one shot at a time." Don't worry about hazards that are two or three shots, or holes, ahead. Deal with the shot in front of you and then move on to the next one.

2. Hazards

So what, generally, makes a golfer nervous? Well, the list is endless but the most common things are water hazards, out-of-bounds, trees, bunkers, and deep rough. Let's address each one individually, but first remember the most important concept of recovery shots: do not follow a bad shot with a dumb one. Try to get the ball back in play, without getting too greedy, and avoid the big number that destroys rounds.

Teach yourself to look forward to tough shots. Having the confidence to play from tough situations comes from practice. Even in casual rounds, don't cheat and roll your ball out of a bad lie. The game is an outdoor sport and is not meant to provide you with a perfect lie every time, even when you hit the fairway. Play the ball where it lies and enjoy the challenge. You will not gain the necessary experience you will need in pressure situations if you avoid the problem in your practice, or casual, rounds.

a. Water

First, let's talk about water hazards. There are two basic types: regular and lateral hazards. Regular water hazards are outlined by yellow stakes or lines painted on the ground. Lateral hazards will be defined by red stakes or lines. Generally speaking, regular water hazards will be more punishing with regard to your drop area and the distance they will cost you. Both hazards carry penalties of only one stroke, but many regular hazards can, effectively, be a penalty of stroke and distance. Lateral hazards will always cost you one stroke but, many times, not much distance, if any at all. Therefore, they're not quite as detrimental to your score. Understanding what a bad shot will cost you is the first step toward making better decisions. Always try to avoid the most costly of all mistakes that are possible.

The best way to overcome your anxiety when faced with a water hazard that comes into play is through the use of positive thinking. The late Harvey Penick, a famous instructor from Texas, used to teach his students to use only positive words and phrases when talking out loud or just to themselves. In other words, don't let the last thoughts before you swing be "<u>Don't</u> hit this in the water." Instead, say to yourself "hit this over the water." Take out the negativity and replace it with a positive swing thought and you will be surprised at the results. Using negative swing thoughts is akin to simply talking yourself into hitting the ball in the water. Similarly, replace thoughts like "don't hit it left" with "hit it right." Get the idea? It's one of the simplest things you'll ever do on a golf course to save yourself strokes.

b. Out Of Bounds

Second, let's discuss out-of-bounds and how to deal with it. Out-of-bounds (OB) will be defined by white stakes or painted lines on the ground, or sometimes a fence. OB is, essentially, the worst penalty you can incur because it costs you both stroke and distance. Lost ball is just as costly but sometimes you can hit a good shot and lose it; with OB, you knew it was there before you hit the ball so it's your fault for hitting it there. So, if you have OB right and water left, you had better make your mistake left and take the right side out of play. The best way to avoid "OB nerves" is in your club selection. Whenever possible, choose a club that will not reach the OB or that you are confident will not go in the direction of the OB markers. If OB is on the right, then use a club you know you never slice or at least one that you're confident you can control the left-to-right movement. You should always have a "go to" club that you can depend on when it's really important. Be willing to give up yardage for the promise of safety.

c. Trees

Third, let's move on to a situation that does not include penalty strokes but can be just as costly, if not more: trees. In American golf, you will encounter trees on nearly every golf course, practically every golf hole, and darn close to every golf shot. They are always lurking around to the right or left of the fairway and rough, and sometimes they're right in the middle of the fairway. They tempt you on the corners of doglegs and hang out in front of some tee boxes. You may play plenty of courses in this country without rough, sand or even water, but trees are nearly everywhere. Why, then, do you never see anyone at the range practicing their recovery shots from the trees? Because nobody thinks about it until they're playing golf and they find themselves standing among the trees wondering how to hit a cut-punch shot to get back to the fairway. Except for scratch amateurs and pros, most golfers will end up hitting one or two more trees before they see daylight again. If you want to overcome your nerves when recovering from the woods, then simply practice hitting low punch shots with your 3, 4 or 5-iron at the range. Practice straight shots as well as cuts and low, running hooks. Then, when you find yourself in the trees again you might actually relish the opportunity to hit a creative, but controlled, recovery shot. That's a big part of what separates Tiger Woods from other PGA Tour pros—when you think he's dead he recovers beautifully.

Personally, I (Matt) like to find objects at the range that I can practice hitting at every time I go to that particular range. Several years ago, I had a favorite spot on my favorite driving range that gave me a good vantage point to practice all of my normal shots, plus a particularly good angle to practice creative recovery shots targeted at a telephone pole that was about 100 yards out. I would end all of my practice sessions by hitting 30 balls at it and hoping to hit it just once. I'd hit 10 low hooks, 10 low cuts, and 10 straight punch shots. On the range I would envision that I was hitting these shots as recoveries from the trees, weaving my way through trouble to safety in the fairway or on the green, represented by the telephone pole. When I reached the golf course and found myself in trouble in the trees, I would do the opposite: I would envision myself at the range comfortably hitting the low, punch recovery shot that I had practiced so often. Eventually, I no longer feared the trees because I was confident that I could recover most of the time. In fact, I grew to love the challenge of working the ball through and around trees. In addition, I reached a point, at the peak of my practice years, that I was hitting that telephone pole an average of 6–7 times for every 30 shots. Golf is much more fun when you play with confidence.

d. Bunkers

Fourth, bunkers can be a traumatic visual for a lot of golfers. Some people are so terrified of bunkers that they will avoid them at all costs. While you definitely want to avoid bunkers, they are usually not the worst place to be and they can still provide scoring opportunities in the right conditions. Some golfers may have no problem with greenside bunkers but get weak in the knees trying to escape from fairway bunkers. Certain courses even present the challenge of huge waste bunkers that are very intimidating. Without question, however, the most penalizing bunker you will encounter is the pot bunker. Fortunately, we don't see too many of them in this country, as it is an attribute usually associated with European courses. They are small, deep and commonly require the golfer to hit his ball out backwards instead of being able to advance it. Avoid pot bunkers at all costs!

The two best tips for conquering your fear of bunkers are really just reviews of the previous advice in this chapter. Referring, again, to Harvey Penick and the power of positive thinking, he never allowed his students to use the term "sand trap" because the word "trap" contains negative connotations. Both mentally and out loud, train yourself to use the word "bunker," instead. The other tip to review is simply to practice, practice, practice. Spend some time in the practice bunker whenever the course you're playing has one available. For fairway bunker practice, you do not need a bunker. When you're at the range just practice hitting balls while keeping your lower body totally quiet. This means no lifting your heels, shifting your hips or any lower body movement, whatsoever. Fairway bunker shots require a swing that is strictly upper body and a still head so that you can pick the ball clean.

e. Deep Rough

The subject of deep rough is fifth on the list. During the course of most casual rounds you will not encounter severe rough very often. Generally, you will only have to deal with rough deeper than two or three inches in tournament play. The reason for this is because the average recreational golfer and country club member will find deep rough to be too frustrating and will not frequent the course. Therefore, most courses keep their rough at a manageable height that allows the golfers to still get a shot to the green. Tournament style rough can be so difficult that the competitors can only wedge the ball back out to the fairway. If you get greedy, 4-inch rough can cost you a stroke or two just like a hazard. This is why so much emphasis is always put on hitting fairways during the U.S. Open and the PGA Championship—two tournaments that are famous for their brutal rough.

Overcoming fear of the rough will start with intelligent course management and confidence in your longer irons. Play smart off the tee and get the ball on the fairway, even if you have to leave a longer approach shot. From there, don't get too aggressive with your long irons. Get the ball on the green and give yourself a chance at birdie or a simple 2-putt par. Almost without exception, a course or tournament with deep rough will also be one where par is always a good score and should keep you in the thick of things if you remain steady and consistent. Low scores on these types of courses are only shot by the hottest golfers with every aspect of their game in the "A+" category.

f. Wind

Water hazards, out-of-bounds, trees, bunkers, and deep rough typically pose the greatest amount of threat to your golf score; therefore, the most pressure on your nerves and fortitude. However, these are fundamental elements built into a golf course by the architect. The one thing that the designer cannot control is the weather, particularly strong wind. Wind can definitely have an affect on your nerves and you need to learn how to deal with it if you expect to play competitive golf. It can even completely change the way a hole, or an entire course, plays. Par-fours that play 3-wood and wedge downwind can play driver and 4-iron into the wind. A strong crosswind can bring hazards and out-of-bounds into play that you would normally have no problem avoiding. Even holes that play shorter because they are downwind can become difficult to score on if the pin is cut up front, just over a bunker or water. It is very difficult to get your ball to stop or spin back when hitting downwind, even with a wedge. Wind will also dry out the greens and make them firmer, thus increasing the difficulty of distance control on your approach shots.

Beating your nerves on windy days requires mental toughness because you **will** get frustrated all day long regarding club selection, and ball control. You have to remain calm, make sharp decisions, and focus on your balance during the swing. Widen your stance, keep your head down and, once you take the club back, forget about the wind and focus on your swing fundamentals. Surprisingly, the most difficult part of your game in the wind is usually putting and not the full swing. It is very easy to get knocked off balance by the wind or it may also blow your putter off line in your backstroke. You also have to account for the wind when judging the line of your putt, especially if the greens are fast.

3. Be Patient and Stay Focused

Additional difficulties on the golf course will include bad lies, hitting from old divots, side-hill lies and hitting within hazard lines where you cannot ground your club. All of these challenges, and many others too numerous to be listed, may cause your pulse rate to increase. You have to learn to be patient on the golf course and stay focused on **each shot**—not just most of them.

PRACTICAL APPLICATIONS:

Know that every sales objection is similar to the overgrown rough, a sand trap or maybe a water hazard. Through preparation you are ready to hit your sales "ball" out of any and all of these hazards and proceed to the close.

In golf you cannot talk your way out of an objection as your ball lays in a hazard, but you can prepare for this moment and be ready to hit the ball into a position to close the sale on this hole (i.e. get the ball onto the green and into the cup).

Chapter 6 Summary

To increase my sales I will _____!!!

To lower my score I will _____!!!

Chapter 7

Closing—Putt for Dough

CONCEPT (Tying sales and golf together): It's time to close the deal. You need a signature on the sales order or the ball in the hole, depending on which game you're playing. By now, you should have done your homework so you should know your customer and their business, as you should also know your putting green. There may be some negotiation left between you and the sale/hole, so this is the time to sum it all up and take your best shot. You give the client/green one more read to be sure and then close the sale or make the putt. If you are not able to close the deal on the first try, at least make sure that you don't leave much work left for your follow up attempt.

WOW!!! You made it to the green and are ready to close the sale. After all, this is why you are here. Putt the ball in the hole.

But beware of the risks and consequences. Try too hard and the ball rolls far past the hole and you may have a difficult, pressure filled return putt. Pick your words and the strength of your stroke carefully. In both sales and golf, you may have difficult ground to make up, just inches from closing. Putt/close weakly and you may never get the ball to the goal. You may have added another stroke, and you did not pick up a sale.

A. Knowledge of Greens

A green is a green. A close is a close. Nothing can be further from the truth. The only thing the same about golf and sales is that they are spelled the same today and tomorrow. A green, as well as a prospect, may contain variables that present challenges that make what you are doing anything but predictable. Knowledge is a great neutralizer of these manageable obstacles.

Sales

1. Closing the Sale—This is Why You are Here!

Great closers are great closers because they know why they are in sales. If not, they would be doing something else for a living. You only make the dollars when you close, anything short of that is, well, watching the other person get the sale. Your mission is to close the sale. Become knowledgeable of the many types of existing closes. Read the books, study the resources provided by your company, learn from the best.

The assumptive close is one of the most effective closes in use. From the time you meet the prospect obtain the mindset that they want and need your product/service. As you progress through the sales cycle they agree with you of their need and your ability to meet that need. They understand the benefits as you highlight them and they acquire from you the very thing needed to fulfill their needs.

Sounds a lot like dating, doesn't it? We will save that for a different book.

2. Close for the Customer In Front of You

Every prospect you meet is different, even though they may appear the same to you. Each prospect has a different background, circumstance, and temperament. In fact, the same prospect may vary from day to day depending on a host of variables, both professional and personal. As a result, the close that worked so well yesterday to get a sale may not work today with a different prospect. While it is important to master every closing technique, it is more important to master every variation of every closing technique. In each instance make the closing presentation natural and your own, not sounding like it came out of a book or manual.

In addition, realize that there are different personality styles. A true professional knows their own personality style and how it fits, or does not fit, with the other personality styles. There are many good study aids (books, cd's, seminars) on the topic of personality styles. Do your homework in this area and see your success grow as a result.

3. An Example of a Close Gone Bad

When I (Peter) first became a professional salesperson I studied books of sales closes daily. After I finished the first part of my formal training I went out and immediately closed my first sale. The next day, very full of myself for the ease at which I had "mastered" selling the previous day, I went confidently into the appointment that I knew would be the second sale of my newfound career.

After giving an excellent presentation I swooped in for the signature, at which point the prospect looked me in the eye and stated while smiling, "Very good Peter, that was the assumptive close. Want to try again?" I couldn't believe my ears. Sitting in front of me was not only a qualified prospect, but an experienced salesperson that recognized me for the green salesperson I was. Not to be outdone, I closed again, only to hear "that was the alternate of choice close, want to try again?" The problem was, every time he asked the question, my profit margin, and therefore, my commission, was dropping accordingly. In the end, I got the sale (he must have felt sorry for me at some point), made very little commission, and learned a valuable lesson of making the sales cycle a natural work for myself, not just canned phrases from some very good books, videos, etc. In the end, this customer bought from me several times, gave me many referrals and became a great mentor. This is a lesson you, too, can profit from in many ways.

Golf

Before you ever make a stroke with your putter, you must have a significant amount of knowledge about golf greens. This includes: grass types, grain, growth patterns, effects of the elements, size differences, pin locations, undulations, speed, firmness and moisture content. Of course, the best way to gain this knowledge is through extensive play and travel. Start paying attention to all of the nuances that greens have to offer. Absorb the information and retain it for comparative purposes at the next course you play. Whenever possible, talk to local golf pros or the superintendent to get some "inside" info on the greens.

1. Grass Types

I will not go into the details of the various types of grass, but you should pay attention to the differences as you travel from region to region. They all play a little differently depending on certain characteristics. Therefore, I will concentrate on the subjects mentioned above that are common to every golf course you will play.

2. Grain

For instance, you should be aware that putts are slower when putting into the grain and faster when putting down grain. Generally, the grass will grow towards nearby water and away from mountains. Also, note that elevated greens will usually be a little faster because the wind and sun dries them out quicker and water drains faster. If you are playing towards the end of the day, the greens will be a little slower due to the day's growth, plus it may be harder to hold your line because of a day's worth of spike marks.

3. Pin Locations

Be conscious of the fact that a hole may be an easy birdie hole one day due to pin location, and then it may dictate that you play for a safe 2-putt par the next day when they move the pin. For example, the Sunday pin locations at #11 and #12 at Augusta come to mind.

Since we want to focus on closing the deal, though, let's talk about these five particular elements to understanding greens: size, undulation, speed, firmness and moisture.

4. Green Size

First, whether a course has small or large greens will affect your approach to your short game. Small greens require more precision with your approach shots but they also mean that every time you're on the green you should have a legitimate chance at making a putt. Plus, you may find yourself with opportunities to chip or pitch a ball in for birdie because, when you miss the green in regulation, you will find yourself closer to the pin than a miss on large greens. Bigger greens mean more room for error on your approach but it puts more pressure on your long putting since you may end up with some putts of 80 feet or more. Don't be surprised to see more 3-putts than you normally average.

5. Undulation

Second, the amount of undulation in the greens is one of the major factors to consider on every putt. With relatively flat greens, your first thought should always be about your distance control with your putter. However, putting surfaces with significant undulation or multiple levels require more attention to the line of your putt. Distance control is still very important but you have to weigh the risk/reward of hitting putts firmer to hold the line or softer and allowing for more break. A firmer stroke is usually a good option for the confident putter because he's not afraid of a 3 to 5-footer coming back. Most golfers prefer to hit it softer, though, and try to leave themselves a tap-in if they miss. It's strictly a matter of personal preference and it's important that you stay within your comfort zone. Not everyone is suited to be a bold putter. The best way to conquer greens with severe undulations starts with your approach to the green. Be aware of the worst places to be on the green, with regard to that day's pin location, and try to hit your approach to the easier spots on the green from which to putt. If you do this more often than not, you will reduce your stress on the greens, considerably.

6. Speed

Third, the speed of the greens is going to be one of the top factors in determining the overall difficulty of the course and your ability to shoot low scores. The reasons it affects you are threefold: 1) distance control with your approach shots; 2) ability to recover for par when you miss the green; and 3) level of aggressiveness with your putting.

Before we cover these three topics, let's make sure that you understand a few standards and fundamentals. Green speed is measured with a stimpmeter, and the resulting measurement is commonly referred to as the stimp or stimp speed of the greens. A stimpmeter is a simple device that, after tests in both directions and multiple locations on the green, provides the average number of feet and inches that a golf ball rolls on the green. So, if you hear that a particular course has their greens running at a speed of 9.5, then that means the average distance the ball rolled from the stimpmeter was 9 feet, 6 inches. Most municipal golf courses around the country keep the greens stimping between 7–10 feet. There are two basic reasons why they don't cut them any shorter: too much foot traffic is hard on greens running faster than 10 feet, and anything faster gets to be a real challenge to play on and your average golfer will not enjoy four-putting all day. Private clubs and high end daily fee courses get less play and golfers expect to get more of a challenging course when they pay more money to play. Therefore, you will find stimp speeds between 8.5 and 11 feet at those courses. Courses hosting top amateur or pro events will rarely have their greens below 10.5 feet, except when high winds are expected because the greens can become unfair in the wind at those stimp speeds.

Most golfers consider slower greens to be easier to handle, but not all. In his book *Every Shot I Take*, Davis Love III notes that his father, Davis Love Jr., taught him to prefer fast greens because, in theory, the faster the green the shorter your putting stroke and, therefore, you should be able to keep your stroke on line much easier. I agree with this theory and I have always enjoyed playing courses with fast greens. Plus, the shorter the grass the truer the roll, so you really just have to get the ball started on line and you have a better chance of making putts. Slower greens mean longer blades and more grain in the grass so putts must be hit firmer to hold their line.

Additional reasons for variation in green speeds from course to course include climate and recent weather conditions, changing seasons, water availability, drainage systems, turf health, insects or disease, greens keeper knowledge and/or preference, and the quality of treatment from the golfers that frequent the course. The list goes on and on but, if you're curious about a particular course, just ask the pro or superintendent for an explanation.

7. Firmness

Fourth, the firmness of the greens is always an issue and is directly related to the discussion we just completed about the speed of the greens. Soft greens will be more receptive to approach shots but you have to be careful with the spin you put on the ball. Back pin locations will be more difficult to get close to, but front pins give you plenty of room to hit past the hole and spin it back. When you get on the green, soft greens will, generally, putt slower but not always so you have to experiment the first few holes.

Firm greens will behave in the opposite manner from the soft greens, essentially. It is harder to spin the ball to a stop, so you have to have target yardage that is short of the pin, allowing for some release. Thus, it is harder to get at front pins and easier to go for the back pins. One big difference, however, is that you must be more careful with your approach shots so as not to short-side (miss the green on the side of the flag) yourself because par saves will be more difficult on firm greens with little room to land the ball. When putting, firm greens should be a little faster but that is not an absolute.

8. Moisture Content

Fifth, and last with regard to green conditions, is the moisture content of the green. In other words, dry greens versus wet ones. Adding moisture to the equation is where it gets a little confusing and you really have to rely on your experience. This is because it is possible to have greens that are wet, firm and fast or dry, soft and fast. Almost any combination of these conditions is possible, although the most common two combinations will be dry, firm and fast, and then wet, soft and slow. Just don't make any assumptions and try to learn as much as you can from the first two or three greens.

B. Negotiation

Very rarely does the ball go straight into the cup or does the prospect insist on signing the order now, no questions asked. There are ways to ensure that the goal is achieved.

Sales

1. Give and Take

As a salesperson, you know what liberties you can and cannot give to a prospect to turn them into a customer. Most prospects, especially experienced or savvy buyers know not only that you can concede on some points but also have a budget figure in mind that must be met before they will buy. The good news is that for the most part everything is negotiable. The bad news is not everything is fully negotiable to totally satisfy everyone. The magic word is compromise. Within the give and take process it is up to you to formulate a win/win solution.

2. Win/Win

The best win/win solutions result in everyone happy and satisfied with the outcome. You get a sale and referrals; the prospect becomes a customer that sings the praises of you and your company. Many times the solution falls short of the stated perfection; you made a sale and the new customer is just happy the selling process is over. It is your job to ensure your follow-up after the sale results in a completely satisfied customer that is bragging about you and your company. Remember, if you have a satisfied customer they may say good things about you, but if you have an unsatisfied customer, they WILL say bad things about you.

Golf

Now that you are armed with a wealth of education about the greens and are ready to try and close the deal, it is time for negotiation. For our purposes, we'll consider putts of 20 feet or less to be "makeable." You will be negotiating two main things: speed and break.

1. Speed vs. Break

Ironically, you can approach the negotiations in one of two ways: 1) let your speed determine how much break you will borrow; or 2) let the break determine your speed. Neither method is better than the other—it is simply a matter of personal preference, you may even toggle between both methods from hole to hole, evaluating each individual situation. If you choose option one, you're choosing to play conservatively and assure an easy 2-putt by leaving the ball within the optimum 18-inch range after the first putt. If you choose option two, then you're taking the aggressive approach and trying to play less break with a firmer putt that, if you miss, may leave a 4-footer coming back. In the end, the negotiations are really up to you in the sense that you can control the direction and speed but the outcome is still left somewhat up to chance. You can do everything right—good read, good stroke and perfect speed—and still hit a spike mark, ball mark, an insect or anything and get knocked off line. Some bad putts may catch the rim of the cup and curl in and some good putts will catch the rim and spin out. It's a frustrating game, at times, but remember that if you hit it just right every putt will break exactly six inches straight down.

2. Makeable Putts (Less than 20 Feet)

As a general rule, great putters use option two and putt aggressively. One major reason is that it will help to eliminate any tentativeness in your putting stroke. Get over your fear of 3-putting by practicing your 3–6 foot putts and then you will not be afraid of taking a good run at an 18-footer. That doesn't mean that it's okay to run every putt by the hole by several feet. You still need to concentrate on your distance control and, when you're not afraid of your second putt, you will be more likely to make your first putt.

Use option one and putt conservatively only in situations where there is a lot of break to be played, it is severely downhill, or if you only need two putts to win, for example.

When I (Matt) was playing competitive golf full time I used to use a psychological technique on myself to help motivate me to make every putt that I stood over that was 10 feet or less. After reading the putt and making a decisive choice as to the break and speed, I would address the ball and repeat the following sentences to myself several times before stroking the putt: "This one's for my daughter. This putt's for my baby girl." My daughter means the world to me so there's no way I was going to let her down by missing a putt that I had dedicated to her. Of course, I did not make every putt, but I guarantee you that I did not miss very often. It is one thing to let yourself down, but when you feel as though someone close to you is depending on you to come through for them you might be surprised as to what you are capable of achieving. Choose someone in your life that you would never want to disappoint and see how it works for you, but don't expect overnight changes. Stick with it and you will see improvement over a period of time.

3. 2-Putts (More than 20 Feet)

Most putts over 20 feet in length are not made with any regularity, so putts from that distance may require a trial close. That means, essentially, that you always maintain some hope that the putt might go in but you don't realistically expect it to fall. It's like a bonus if they do go in, but you don't want to be depending on putts of that length for the bulk of your score. The smart choice is to concentrate on your speed so that you don't leave a lot of work for the second putt—thus making your actual close a simple one.

PRACTICAL APPLICATIONS:

Just as every green has hills and curves, so does every sale. You are ready to 1 putt; maybe 2 putt the ball to close the sale. Always keep your eye on the goal, sink the ball and close the sale.

As you stand over the ball on the putting green, remember that this "sale" is yours, you prepared for it and as a result you are in position to close this sale by putting your ball into the cup. Do it confidently and do it now.

Chapter 7 Summary

To increase my sales I will _____!!!

To lower my score I will _____!!!

Chapter 8

Evaluation and Follow-Up—Measuring Success

CONCEPT (Tying sales and golf together): Just because you closed the sale or finished the hole, or round, does not mean that your job is done. First, you need to evaluate your performance and make sure that you did your job right. While being focused on money can be a great motivator, you may also place a lot of importance on other factors, like personal pride and the prestige associated with being a top performer.

As a salesperson or a golfer, it is necessary to remind yourself to stay focused on the present and do not start thinking too far ahead about plans for successes that you are yet to achieve. Your success will ultimately be measured by your longevity in your field, and that requires repeat performances on a consistent basis. Stay determined and remember to keep doing what you brought success in the first place.

I have made the sale; I have finished my round of golf. What's next? Read on to discuss the most often ignored part of the game.

A. Making the Cut

In sales and in golf it is so important to make the cut. If you don't make the cut you earn a new title: spectator. (Actually it is loser, but that is so cruel. Or is it? What motivates you?)

Sales

1. Sale/No Sale

There is no such thing as getting paid to almost make the sale. You either made the sale or you did not make the sale. The sale is usually made when the paperwork is signed and the customer accepts delivery of the product/service and the back-out time allowed has passed. Then, you have a sale. I think we have all heard sales people tell their managers that they have a sale, only to learn the paperwork has not been signed yet. As bad as it sounds, just because the prospect said they would buy from you does not mean they will buy from you. Many a prospect will say whatever they need to say to get the salesperson away from them. Sad, but true.

2. The Sale is Only Lost When ...

Whenever a prospect tells you they are going to buy from a competitor, ask if they have signed the paperwork AND accepted delivery of the product or service. If they have not met those conditions you have not yet lost the sale. If you want this sale, find out why they are considering the competitor, get your resources together and immediately go see the prospect. Get signed paperwork. Deliver your goods. Get the sale!!!

3. Making Them Your Customer for Life

While it is always great to get a sale, it is most important to win a relationship. Almost every product/service must be acquired again after a certain amount of time. Additionally, a customer may naturally want to get a new product/service after an amount of time. When the "itch cycle" for your product/service/customer starts again you want to be the one to satisfy their itch by buying again from you. It may be one of your easiest sales. They know, like and trust you if you did it right the first time. Why wouldn't they buy from you again?

Whenever you win a new customer, let them know you are looking forward to a long and mutually beneficial relationship.

Golf

For most professionals, just making it to the big time (i.e. PGA Tour) is a major accomplishment. However, if you can't make the cut and play on the weekends then you're really just another wallflower at the dance. Most golfers will never know the pressure of standing over a putt worth hundreds of thousands of dollars or, at the mini-tour level, worth enough to pay your rent or electric bill. For the journeymen, it is possible to play weeks on end where you're only earning enough money to pay your expenses for the tournament and get you to the next one. It is nerve wracking, to say the least, but you're still doing what you love so you find a way to deal with the pressure.

Nothing ... absolutely nothing ... matters if you do not make the cut. Playing professional golf is all about making money. It's a career just like any other. Everyone wants to make a good living and support their family. There are a select few in the world that don't ever have to worry about money, but most pros always have their paycheck somewhere in the back of their mind. Unlike other sports where you sign a contract for a salary, pro golfers do not get paid unless they make the cut, except for endorsement money but that, too, will soon disappear if you're not making cuts.

1. Saturday

So, now you've got two good rounds under your belt and you're playing the weekend. In a four-day tournament, Saturday is commonly referred to as "moving day." It earned that name because there is usually a lot of shifting on the leader board—players moving up and others moving down the board. All of the pressure of making the cut is over so a lot of competitors start playing more aggressively and going for low scores.

2. Sunday

By Sunday morning, everyone pretty much knows if they have a chance to win the tournament or not. The players who do have a chance are the ones who might start feeling the pressure; whereas, everyone else can enjoy a pressure-free round and just try to earn as big of a check as possible. Also, on the PGA Tour and other top tours around the world, top-20 finishes earn world ranking points which help players qualify for many other tournaments. So, there are still things to play for even if you don't have a chance to win the tournament.

B. Playing for More than Just Money

There are many reasons to play the game. Money aside, let's look at a few of the many reasons.

Sales

1. Networking—Give Your Customer Some Business

All of us have a network of personal and professional relationships. Whether you realize it or not, your prospects, customers, and you have one very important thing in common—all of you need customers. What better way to solidify your relationships with your customers than to give them business? Learn who the target markets are for your customers and give them business contacts that can turn into money for them. Not only will they like you more, but it will set you apart from your competitors.

2. Referrals—Give Yourself Some Business

Now that you have given your customers some business you can ask for referrals confidently. After all, you are creating win/win scenarios. Find out who are your customers' favorite customer or vendor. Also, ask about their neighbors. Your next customer may be on the other side of the wall. Make it your goal to get so many referrals that you do not have time to make cold calls.

Golf

1. Pride

For the competitors playing well enough to be in the hunt on Sunday, there are many thoughts racing through their mind including money, prestige, exemptions, endorsements and pride. Golfers all play for different reasons, but pride is the one common denominator from the PGA Tour all the way down to local club championships. Some people play to make their father or mother proud, and others play to make their spouse or kids proud of them. Many golfers compete for their own personal pride and others may be competing for the pride of their club or school. Whatever, or whomever, it is that gives you motivation is not important, but is it important to be playing for something or someone that means something to you. If you are without motivation then you're wasting your time and probably wasting your money on entry fees and travel expenses.

Back in my (Matt) amateur days, I will never forget the way people began to look at me after I won my first club championship at my home course. I went from being a "nobody" at the course to being recognized when I arrived, pointed at by curious bystanders and introduced by the starter as the "club champion." All of a sudden, I had some kind of minor celebrity status amongst my peers. It was a public course run by the city and so the club hosted an annual dinner for the club champions (men's, ladies', and senior's division winners) and we were presented our trophies by the mayor. My wife was very proud of me, as was my father and mother, and I was very proud of myself and what I had achieved. The only thing that felt better than that was when I won again the following year and cemented my legacy at that golf course for as long as it continues to exist.

2. Prestige

A tournament win is a trophy on the mantle and bragging rights for a year. On the PGA Tour, you're also etching your name in history. Your name might be on the same trophy with the likes of Byron Nelson, Sam Snead, Ben Hogan, Jack Nicklaus, or Arnold Palmer. That is an indescribable feeling and a tremendous sense of accomplishment. Even at the local amateur level, you may get your name on the same title that the best golfers in your state's history have shared.

Some of the most prestigious tournaments on the PGA Tour are those that have a long-standing tradition and an impressive list of past winners. Setting aside the majors and relatively new tournaments, every golfer on tour has tournaments like the Western Open, Colonial, Bay Hill and the Memorial on their list of "most important" tournaments every year. A win at any of those tournaments carries significant prestige and garners the immediate respect of your peers and fans and helps elevate your image to a new level.

At the local and state level, the most prestigious tournaments might be your club championship, city championship, state open, state amateur, state mid-amateur or the public links championship. You may even find your name on the same trophy with former amateurs who went on to well-respected professional careers.

C. Don't Get Ahead of Yourself

Have you ever watched a race on TV in which the leader has a sizeable lead? Have you ever watched in horror as he or she loses the race at the finish line because they did not run the race to the very end, but only to 99.9% of the race? Remember, it's not over until it's over.

Sales

1. A Sale is Not a Sale Until …

As we have already discussed, a sale is not a sale until you have signed paperwork, delivery of your product/service is complete and the customer's right of refusal time has passed. As a sales professional be sure to be thorough in the latter stages of a sale. If a prospect says they will buy from you but will not memorialize the transaction with a signed contract, you do not have a sale, you have a wish.

2. Don't Spend It Before You Get It

Unfortunately, many sales people take these wishes, figure how much money they would make on this wish, and then spend the commission before they ever received it. Do not spend money before it is in your bank account. You cannot pay your expenses with "wish dollars."

Likewise, sometimes sales managers prefer the members of their sales teams to have many financial obligations such as a mortgage, cars, boats, etc. so they have pre-existing financial incentive to succeed. However you do it, make sure you do not live above your means. Utilize your career in sales to improve your lifestyle as defined by you.

Golf

1. Stay in the Moment

Victory is always sweet, no matter what level at which you compete. To get there, though, be sure to remain in the moment while coming down the stretch.

2. Anything Can Happen Until the Last Putt Drops

Don't get ahead of yourself and start planning your victory speech when you still have three holes to play. If you need an example of the fact that anything can happen, simply look back a few years to Jean Van de Valde at the 1999 British Open at Carnoustie. All he needed was a double bogey on the 72nd hole to win the tournament but he made a triple bogey, and had to make a difficult sand save for that score! He let Justin Leonard and Paul Lawrie back into the tournament and had to go to a playoff with them, which was eventually won by Lawrie. It was an enormous mental mistake more than a physical bad swing. He had an opportunity to play safe and make an easy bogey for the win but he went for the glory shot to finish with birdie or par that he didn't even need. It was a tragic end to an otherwise impressive tournament, and nobody remembers how well he played the first 71 holes of that Open Championship. **Do not** get ahead of yourself or assume that you have the event wrapped up. Anything can happen until the last putt drops.

Victory is what we all play for, though. Enjoy it but be humble in your celebration. Remember, no victory ever assures you of another one. There are as many one-tournament winners in PGA Tour history as there are one-hit wonders on the Billboard music charts. Savor your win and then quickly begin working on the next one. No matter how many times you win, never be satisfied. That mindset will keep driving you to more wins. The true measure of success is time.

D. Don't be a "One-Hit Wonder"

Nothing in life is just a one time event; the feeling of joy, accomplishment, car payments, etc. Each is repeated over and over and over … With that in mind, why not decide that your success in sales and golf will be a continual occurrence, not just a one time anomaly.

Sales

1. Job vs. Career

Many people try a sales job, and then wonder why they failed. A job is something you do just to get a paycheck; a career is something you do because you are passionate about it. In a job you learn how to do things. In a career you learn how to do things, why you do them, and how to do them better than anyone else. Sales can be your career choice. Mastering every aspect of the sales cycle will make you a sales professional. The product or service you sell is the vehicle utilized to generate the income. By understanding this you increase your chances at avoiding the label of "one hit wonder."

2. Burnout

The opposite of burnout is balance. To avoid burnout be sure to maintain balance in every part of your personal and professional life. When you plan your goals, be sure they address every aspect of your life and are evenly weighted between the personal and professional parts of your life.

Another cause of burnout is just being in the wrong profession. Take an inventory of your strengths and weaknesses to ensure you are working in the right field.

Golf

1. Follow Up/Repeat Performance

The best way to help you avoid being a one-hit wonder is to follow up your great performance with good, hard-working practice sessions that reinforce the mechanics that brought you success. Keep driving yourself forward and do not fall into the trappings of laziness just because you're sitting on a big paycheck. Use your success to build more successes and you'll soon be enjoying the spoils of a repeat performance of your victory. Be sure to make note of what you did differently to become a winner. Usually, it's just a couple of small details that you managed to work out and everything began clicking with your game, but it is important to identify what they are and focus on them during your practice sessions. Most people tend to practice only when their swing is giving them problems. It's just as important to practice when you're swinging good because then you are developing the muscle memory that created your winning swing.

E. Measuring Success

Your success can be measured by you or by those around you. The problem with sales and golf is that there is never perfection, just degrees of success. Let's explore some of the ways in which you can experience the satisfying feeling of success.

Sales

If you truly want to keep score of your sales in a golf format, here it is:

1. Sales **Par**	You made the sale.
2. Sales **Birdie**	You made the sale and got referrals.
3. Sales **Eagle**	You made the sale and got referrals that the customer called for you to make an introduction of you and your company.
4. Sales **Bogey**	You made the sale but it took too many calls to close the sale.

5. Sales **Double Bogey**	You lose the sale.
6. Sales **Triple Bogey**	You lose the sale and the prospect tells you and/or others how bad you and your company are.

Look at your next 18 calls and score your sales cycle proficiency in a golf format. See Appendix III to fill out your scorecard.

7. $$$$$ Earned

Some people like to measure success in terms of the money they take home. It is a very tangible measurement of success. Can you ever get enough money? Our advice is to set your goals, achieve those goals, and keep a balanced lifestyle.

8. $$$$$ Sold

Companies usually report their total sales in their income statements. As a sales professional you should know what percentage of the company sales are attributed to you. Make it a goal to be the top producer for your company. The more your company relies on your track record of success, the better your negotiating position for better pay, benefits, bonuses, perks, and promotion.

Also, please keep in mind to maintain profitability in your sales. There is not much to be said if you are selling your product or service at a margin that costs the company money rather than profiting the company.

9. Units Sold

Another measure of success is based on the number of units you sell in a given time. Again, make it your mission to sell more units at a given profit margin than anyone in your company.

10. Closing Ratio

The better your closing ratio, the more efficiently and easier you have to work. You can calculate your closing ratio by dividing the number of presentations you make by the number of times you actually close the sale. Research your industry to see if your closing ratio is better or worse than the average salesperson. Then master the sales cycle to become much better than the average salesperson in your industry.

11. The Most Important Measure of Daily Success in Sales

In spite of all the ways we have mentioned to measure success, the truest way to measure your daily success in sales is to plant a given number of sales "seeds" everyday through prospecting. The daily number of contact will be based upon your industry standards and on your ambition to succeed. Every seed you plant today has the potential to blossom at any given time. At the end of every sales day ask yourself this very important question, "Do more people right now know that I am selling _____ than at 8:00 a.m. this morning?" If the answer is yes and you know that you contacted everyone you were capable of, then feel satisfied. The rewards will come. You are a master of the sales cycle.

By doing this you will find your stress level lower and you will be able to make more sales. Prospects can tell if you are under stress to make a sale. Prospects can also tell if you are relaxed and enjoy the sales process. Which type of salesperson would you buy from? Be the salesperson you would like to spend your hard earned money with.

Golf

1. Time is the True Measure

As I noted above, the true measure of your success will be time. There are tons of great golfers that have dominated the PGA Tour for a few years, but only a handful has been able to stand the test of time. Jack Nicklaus is the best example of this principle. His unbelievable dominance reigned over the Tour for almost three decades. Even Tiger Woods would tell you that he is nowhere near being the greatest golfer ever because he is not old enough to have proven that he can stand the test of time yet. Just about everyone believes that he will break Nicklaus' record of 18 professional majors someday, but the one thing he needs to accomplish that feat is time. Nicklaus won his last major at the Masters at the age of 46. While he has accomplished success at an unbelievable rate so far, Woods still has a long way to go to be the greatest golfer of all time.

Hale Irwin is another great modern day example of enduring talent and determination. He was a great player on the regular tour, but he has been the best ever on the Champions Tour and still continues to win. Sam Snead was another legend that continued to amaze fans with his level of play well into his 50's on the PGA Tour. In contrast, look at players such as Johnny Miller or David Duval who were the best in the world at one time but then completely lost their game. Duval is beginning to play better but time will only tell if he'll ever regain his previous brilliance and be a star again. Miller inexplicably won at Pebble Beach in the mid-90's but, other than that, his game completely deserted him decades ago, although he has always remained an excellent ball-striker with his irons.

2. Determination

If you are determined not to be a "one-hit wonder" then you must keep setting your goals higher and, when you achieve them, set them higher again. The process of setting and achieving goals is what truly drives any competitor. Think of it this way: pro golfers are not content to simply hit the fairway off the tee. Instead, they want to find a particular side of the fairway at a specific distance so that they have their desired angle and yardage for their next shot. Comparatively, if you enter a tournament just to play and see how you do with no expectations, then you might as well be standing on the tee and just be hoping to hit some grass somewhere out there. You must set specific goals that drive you to constantly achieve results at a higher level. The determined golfer will eventually achieve his goals.

3. Keep Doing What Got You There and Don't Slack Off When You Become Successful.

Once you have found a formula for success, keep using it until it doesn't work anymore or until you find an even better formula that will take you to the next level. Never be satisfied and always know that, just because you know a lot and have achieved results at a very high level, you can always learn more and do better.

The point is this: do not ever think that, because you're on top now, you will always be on top. Stay focused on your goals and be aware that there will always be someone coming up the ranks that desire to be in your position. To be great you must stand the test of time.

PRACTICAL APPLICATIONS:

There is no such thing as perfection, in sales or in golf. Keep a fresh approach to both by exploring the parallels of sales and golf. Understand each until they are second nature to you. By doing this you will find that the victories experienced in sales, carry over to golf, and visa versa.

Chapter 8 Summary

To increase my sales I will _____!!!

To lower my score I will _____!!!

Chapter 9

Keeping Score

CONCEPT (Tying sales and golf together): There are many ways to keep score in both sales and golf. In sales, you have a base salary but the focus is usually on commissions, bonuses, awards and other incentives. In golf, the focus is most commonly on medal play, also known as stroke play. However, you may also find opportunities to compete in match play, best ball or scramble events, among others.

While there are many ways to keep score and/or compete, there is always a way to determine who is the winner and who is not. Hopefully, you will be the winner more often than not. If so, the money and the awards will begin to pile up.

Let's look at both sales and golf as a game. The fun thing about games is that there are several ways to keep score. Let's find a format that you enjoy and profit from the most.

Sales

1. Salary Plus Commission

Salary plus commission gives you some security of a regular paycheck by sacrificing for a smaller commission. This is great if you are new to sales and wanting to learn what you are really capable of. Enjoy it while you can.

2. Commission Only

Many times a commission only situation means you are an agent or some other type of non-employee to the company. As a result, you usually receive a premium commission on the sales you make. This is great for a seasoned, and secure, sales professional. Amateurs need not apply.

When I (Peter) first came into sales, the president of the company I worked for had a sign in his office that had lasting impact. It boldly proclaimed: "Your Raise Becomes Effective As Soon As You Do."

If you receive any form of commission, that is your creed.

3. Bonuses

Bonuses are a reward when you go above and beyond a stated goal. Bonuses are not a part of doing sub-par work. This is said because so many salespeople want bonuses just for showing up. A bonus is an extra. Appreciate it in that form.

4. Benefits

If you are an employee of a company you may be eligible for medical, dental, and life insurance. There may also be retirement benefits and a 401K retirement savings plan. In many instances, the company will match a certain percentage of your 401K contributions. Paid time off (PTO) may also be rewarded or accrued for vacation or sick time.

5. Perks

Perks include cars, mileage allowances, meal money and golf outings, etc. Use your imagination here but, while you are imagining, take a realistic look at the resources your company has available. The great thing about sales is that while you are making a lot of sales, which translates into money for your company, you can negotiate some perks as you are comfortable.

6. Travel

Company travel does not mean taking a vacation at the company's expense. Realize that, when your company sends you someplace, it is for a specific purpose with a desired result, usually a sale. Show your company you are a sales professional by representing them well while on the road.

7. Awards

Companies love to give awards to salespeople and salespeople love to receive awards. Learn about all the awards you are eligible for and make it a goal to earn those awards. Sometimes there are some great perks that accompany an award.

8. Contests

Contests are usually utilized by companies to assist in motivating salespeople and stimulating sales. Realize that sales contests are a type of external motivation. As a sales professional, be sure you are internally motivated by your own goals and priorities. An internally motivated salesperson will beat an externally motivated salesperson the majority of the time in a contest situation. Make it your goal to win every sales contest.

Golf

1. Medal (Stroke) Play

The most common form of golf that everyone plays is medal, or stroke, play. This is simply totaling up your strokes every hole and then another total after 18 holes that gives you your final score. Other forms of golf include match play, best ball, alternate shot, scrambles, long drive contests and team golf such as high school or college. Each one brings its own elements to the game and encourages a different approach, from a tactical standpoint and sometimes a mental one.

2. Match Play

Match play is seen a couple of times every year on the PGA Tour during the World Golf Championships and the Ryder Cup or President's Cup. It can be found, however, every day at local golf courses where friends play each other for skins, nassaus and many other forms of gambling. In match play, you may still keep a medal score but the winner is not determined by the total number of strokes after 18 holes. Instead, match play determines a winner on a hole by hole basis, and then the winner is determined by who won more holes out of the total played. So, in essence, every hole starts a new mini-tournament. If you make a triple bogey in medal play you lose three strokes and that can be devastating to your score. In match play, you would only lose that one hole and you could turn around and win the next hole and be all square again. Therefore, your mental approach needs to be different. If your competition has already made par and you are left with a 20-foot putt for par, then don't even think about getting the putt close—the only thing that matters is **making** the putt. If it goes six feet by the hole you don't have to putt the next one because it doesn't mean anything—you've already lost the hole.

There are a lot of mental games that you play in match play too. You can get inside your competitor's psyche and put more pressure on him. Ben Hogan used to lay back shorter off the tee on purpose so he could hit his approach first and make the other guy have to look at his ball on the green when it was his turn. You can choose to concede three-foot putts to your competitor all day until it matters at the end of the round and then make him putt one when the pressure is on. There are many subtle ways to grind away at your competitor because he's the only one you're playing against—not the entire field.

Your course management may change, as well. If your competitor tees off first and hits a ball in the water, then change your game plan and hit a safe club off the tee since par, or even bogey, will probably win the hole. If you're playing well, then it's usually advantageous to be hitting first so you can apply pressure to your competitor. However, if your game is a little suspect, then hitting second can provide some opportunities to play more conservatively.

Although I (Matt) have been able to develop a little more length off the tee in the last couple of years, I have never been known as a long hitter. My competitors, however, have always known me to be someone who hits a lot of fairways and saves a lot of pars around the greens. These are two features of my game that have always made me a tough competitor in match play because I keep the ball in play and don't give away holes due to penalty strokes, and when I miss greens my competitors still figure they need birdie to beat me because they expect me to get up and down for par. This puts a lot of extra pressure on your opponent when they know that you will rarely ever beat yourself and that they are going to have to make birdies to win holes. When competing in the match play format, the best way to wear down your opponent is to consistently hit fairways and greens, never bringing bogey into play, and occasionally making a putt for birdie. Your opponent will have to possess some strong mental fortitude to overcome your simple consistency all day. I can recall many matches in my career where I was a much shorter hitter and considered the underdog but I prevailed by playing my own game and forcing my opponent to play his best golf to beat me.

Match play, also, does not always last the full 18 holes. You may have heard terms such as "2 and 1" or "4 and 3." This means that the winner was ahead by two holes with only one to play, effectively ending the match on the 17th green, or by four holes with three to play which would end the match on the 15th green.

A winning score of "1 up" means that the match went 18 holes and the winner either started the last hole one up and tied the hole or he won the 18th for a one hole victory. Another common term is "dormie." This occurs when, for example, a player is two holes down with two to play. He is dormied because the best he can do is winning the last two holes for a tie in the match or to go to extra holes, depending on the tournament format. When you win a match play round it is referred to as having "closed out" your opponent.

3. Best Ball

Although not required to be, best ball events are usually 2-man formats. In these events, each player on a 2-man team plays his own ball throughout each hole for a medal score. The team score, however, is the better of the two scores. In other words, if I score a five and my partner scores a four, then our team score for the hole is four. In some amateur tournaments where handicaps are used, my partner's four might also be a "net 3" with his handicap, so then our team score would be three. The best ball format can be used in a medal tournament for total scores, or we might be using our best ball score in a match play event against the other two man team in our foursome.

4. Alternate Shot

An alternate shot format is always interesting because of the challenges that face each golfer when trying to recover from their partner's mistake. Alternate shot is a two man format where both players tee off and then they choose the best ball and play the rest of the hole taking turns with one ball. In other words, my partner and I choose to play his tee shot so I hit our second shot, he hits our third, I hit our fourth and so on until the ball is holed out. This type of event can also be played where, instead of two tee shots, one player tees off on all odd-numbered holes and the other tees off on even-numbered holes only. These events are interesting because you have to not only know your game very well, but also your partner's. If you know that your partner's bunker game is weak then you have to make sure to take all bunkers out of play when you hit. Conversely, if you have a strong partner who can muscle balls out of deep rough, then you can swing more freely on the tee and not worry too much about missing the fairway.

5. Scramble

The tournament format that every golfer knows well is the scramble. Most golfers play in, at least, two or three scrambles every year. The beauty of the scramble is that, if you hit a bad shot, you don't have to play it. Scrambles are most commonly played as four man team events, but can also be a two man format. In a scramble event, each member of the team tees off and the best ball is then chosen. The other balls are picked up and placed within a club-length of the chosen best ball. Then, all team members play their next shot from that spot. This procedure continues until the ball is holed out. These events can be fun for players of all levels because even a 25-handicapper can contribute to the team with some good putts or consistent 3-irons off the tee to be sure of always having a ball in the fairway. The ideal team will consist of a long hitter, a good putter, a straight hitter and a solid iron player that almost always finds the green with his approach shots. For the long hitter, scrambles are fun because they can "swing away" on every par-4 and par-5 and not worry about having to play a ball from the trees. For the other team members, they get a chance to play from spots on the course that they don't normally get to see. For instance, hitting wedge to a green that they normally have to use a 5-iron to reach.

Scrambles also include some fun elements like closest-to-the-pin contests on the par-3's and a longest-drive hole, as well as a straightest-drive hole. Plus, sometimes you can buy mulligans for $5 or $10 each, and then use them where you need to on the course. The money is usually all going to charity or some worthy fundraising effort, so get involved and have some fun.

6. School Teams

Another form of team golf is organized golf such as high school and college teams. In these events, there are usually five starting golfers that make up each squad and they each compete as if they were playing their own medal play tournament. At the end of each day, the top four scores are totaled up for the team score and the highest round from the team is discarded. So, if four players shoot 70 and the other shoots 75, the 75 is discarded and the team score the day is 280. The most important reason for being there is the team score; however, there is also an individual medal play event taking place. Therefore, it is common to have an individual winner whose team didn't even place in the top five because the rest of their team did not play very well.

7. Long Drive Contests

One very different type of golf that we will discuss is the long drive contest. These are events that take place at the practice range or on one particular hole on the course that has, at least, 400 yards of open fairway. Long drive competitors travel from city to city just like touring pros to compete in these contests that require the ability to drive a ball distances of 325–415 yards. Depending on the wind direction and weather conditions, most of these events will be won with a drive of 350–390 yards. The contestants will have swing speeds ranging from 125mph to 170mph, which creates an incredible amount of ball speed at launch. Generally, they use custom made clubs with longer shafts and heads with loft as low as 4 degrees.

Each contestant is given five attempts to hit their longest ball that stays within a designated fairway, usually about 50 yards wide. All drives outside the lines are not counted, regardless of how far they travel. Long drive contests are exciting to watch because you get to see some monster drives that you would rarely ever see while playing your normal weekend golf at your local municipal course. Many of the competitors will actually be very good golfers on the course, too, but some of them actually play very little, if any, golf. They practice strictly on their tee shots and spend more time in the gym getting stronger and more flexible. Driving the golf ball is an entire sport to them.

8. Practice Rounds

Lastly, there is another type of golf that is rarely discussed or instructed: practice rounds. For professional and top level amateur tournaments, the course will designate days and times available for the competitors to play practice rounds and get prepared for the tournament. During these rounds it is important to hit multiple mulligans to get a sense of different results and how you can handle them during tournament play. You should be much more relaxed and feeling no pressure. You want to get an idea of carry distances, blind shots (find aiming points,) and when more/less club is needed for elevation changes. On the greens, putt to several pin positions, using your best judgment as to where they might be placed during the tournament. Basically, you are not really keeping a score; instead, the objective is to get to know the course as well as you can in one or two days before the tournament.

PRACTICAL APPLICATIONS:

With variety comes a renewal of love for the task at hand, whether it be sales or golf. The "games" you play within each game are transferable and can be enjoyed in both the settings of the office and the golf course. Be creative in both settings and enjoy the mental and physical rewards.

Chapter 9 Summary

To increase my sales I will _____!!!
To lower my score I will _____!!!

Chapter 10

The Salesperson and the Golfer—Our Story Ends

When the salesperson and the golfer had finished exchanging this volume of information they were not just excited, but felt renewed as if they had heard everything about sales and golf for the very first time. The salesperson couldn't wait to get to the golf course as it was clear that improving a bad golf game is as easy as using the sales principles that, in the past, had guaranteed much success. The golfer was so excited to share what appeared to be a wealth of information as to how he and his company could finally reach its full sales potential.

If you are in sales, be a top producer and earn the right to take the time to play and enjoy your golf game.

If you are a golfer, know that the principles that make you a top performing golfer can also make you a top producing salesperson.

And if you are both a salesperson and a golfer, know that as you sell you can reach success by relating all that you do to your golf game and that, while on the golf course, the sales cycle will aid you in lowering your golf score.

After all, everything you need to know about sales you can learn by playing golf!

Postlude

(A Real Life Experience)

One day the salesperson and the golfer actually played a round of golf together. The salesperson was amazed at the proficiency of the golfer. Many years of practice produced long, beautiful shots off the tee, excellent approach shots and putts that actually found the bottom of the cup. But what the salesperson remembered most was a shot that showed the potential of what one can achieve with proper vision, preparation and practice, whether in sales or in golf.

After witnessing another wonderful tee shot by the golfer, the salesperson noticed that there was a very large tree in the middle of the fairway that stood directly between the golf ball and the green. The ball was about ten yards away from the large tree and the green was about 200 yards on the other side of the tree. The salesperson thought that this was a beautiful "take your medicine and punch it out sideways" opportunity for the golfer. After all, laying up was the approach he would take. The golfer explained that he was going to hit the ball around the tree and onto the green **in one shot**. Upon hearing this plan the salesperson laughed, knowing that that was (for him) an impossible shot!!!

The ball ended up about ten feet from the hole.

Appendix

A. My Sales/Golf Evaluation:

On a scale of 1–10, with 10 being perfect, evaluate the following aspects of your sales cycle expertise and your golf game execution:

Sales		Golf	
Preparation	_____	Preparation	_____
Prospecting	_____	Tee Shot	_____
Qualifying	_____	See the Green	_____
Presentation	_____	Approach Shot	_____
Objections	_____	Hazards	_____
Closing	_____	Putting	_____
Follow-Up	_____	Evaluation	_____

Sales Comments:
_____
_____
_____

Golf Comments:
_____
_____
_____

Evaluate yourself on a monthly basis. Additionally, have someone that you trust perform the evaluation of you. Solicit constructive feedback.

B. My Summary

Information transferred from the end of each chapter.

	To increase my sales I will:	**To lower my score I will:**
Preparation	_____	_____
Prospecting/Tee shot	_____	_____
Qualifying/See the green	_____	_____
Presentation/Approach shot	_____	_____
Objections/Hazards	_____	_____
Closing/Putting	_____	_____
Follow-up/Evaluation	_____	_____

Comments:
_____
_____
_____
_____

C. My Sales Scorecard

Sales **Par**	You made the sale
Sales **Birdie**	You made the sale and got referrals
Sales **Eagle**	You made the sale and got referrals that the customer called for you to make an introduction of you and your company
Sales **Bogey**	You made the sale but it took too many calls to close the sale
Sales **Double Bogey**	You lose the sale
Sales **Triple Bogey**	You lose the sale and the prospect tells you and/or others how bad you and your company are

Par 72 (make a sales scorecard based on 18 calls)

Sale #	Par	Score
1	_____	_____
2	_____	_____
3	_____	_____
4	_____	_____
5	_____	_____
6	_____	_____
7	_____	_____
8	_____	_____
9	_____	_____
Sub-Totals	_____	_____

Sale#	Par	Score
10	_____	_____
11	_____	_____
12	_____	_____
13	_____	_____
14	_____	_____
15	_____	_____
16	_____	_____
17	_____	_____
18	_____	_____
Sub-Totals	_____	_____
Totals	_____	_____

About the Authors

Peter Biadasz (pronounced *bee-ahd-ish*) has been a successful and award winning salesperson for over two decades. During this time, Peter has also been working with networking groups in various capacities including president, consultant, and speaker as well as a very active member. As a presenter, Peter not only shares his vision for each organization and business he addresses but carefully leads others to fulfill the vision in a manner that creates win/win scenarios to assist in reaching the goals of each organization. Having taught sales, leadership and networking skills numerous times, Peter has been known to utilize his professional trumpet talent to liven up speaking engagements.

A graduate of Florida State University, Peter's passion for and expertise in the areas of sales and the networking of people has aided many people in getting more leads for their businesses and from their networking activities.

As a golfer, Peter enjoys the game tremendously and is improving. Peter gets his money's worth every time he plays by ensuring he sees much of the course, not so much by shot selection, but by shot execution.

The father of an incredible son and precious daughter, Peter is also the author of *MORE LEADS: The Complete Handbook for TIPS Groups, Leads Groups, and Networking Groups* and co-author of *the Power Series Books*, which include book topics such as networking, teaching, leadership, relationships and listening, to name a few. Please visit with Peter at www.getmoreleads.net or to see the entire list of Power Series titles visit www.bepowerful.net.

Matt Eidson was born and raised in the Midwest and is a graduate of Arizona State University. He began his sales career over 13 years ago in the wedding industry, which allowed him the necessary time to work on his golf game. After competing in amateur golf tournaments with significant success, he turned pro at the age of 29 and competed at the mini-tour level for a little over two years where he managed to win four times. He then worked in the golf industry for a few years, selling everything from golf clubs and accessories to golf nets, mats and artificial putting greens. He is still working in sales and marketing and plays golf with friends, recreationally. Matt's golf skills are completely self-taught as he has never had a single lesson, an accomplishment that he attributes to reading the books of the greatest players and instructors that the game has ever known. He has a beautiful daughter and two incredible sons.

Matt is also co-author of *Powerful People Play Powerful Golf.* That volume of the "Power Series" is a daily guide to improving your golf game through inspirational perspectives and hands-on techniques. Please visit Matt at www.matteidson.com.

Copyright 2007 Peter Biadasz and Matt Eidson

More Of What People Are Saying

"Bring the best of two worlds that belong together: Peter Biadasz's time tested sales and networking skills along with Matt Eidson's insight and passion for golf, and his experience as a pro golfer"

    William Briggs—Financial Associate, for a top Brokerage Firm

"I believe there are few people (Peter and Matt) more knowledgeable on the subjects of networking and golf. I am still absorbing/learning from each one of them."

    Chuck Stikl—Business Owner

"Peter Biadasz obviously has mastery of the sales cycle. Peter offers much practical information to assist anyone who wants to experience greater success."

    R. Possett, Business Owner

"There are many good athletes and businesspeople in the world today, but what separates the good ones from the "Great" ones is how they laboriously and methodically maneuver in their own fields of play. Matt does an excellent job of explaining in a unique and simple perspective how to overcome or just plain avoid the *hazards* that lie ahead. If you are serious about becoming one of the "Great" ones, then take these lessons and apply them to your game."

  J. Smith, *former Northeastern State University Golfer, retired UKF U.S. Super Lightweight Kickboxing Champion and current Commercial Real Estate Broker and Developer*

"Peter Biadasz is a highly focused individual with a high level of energy. What I like best about Peter is that he is not just a talker he is a doer."

J. Weese, District Sales Manager

(See inside front cover for more endorsements)

978-0-595-43783-2
0-595-43783-4